In *Battle Fatigue*, occupational therapist Andrea Patrick, a civilian until she willfully joins the Army, writes about her two deployments to Iraq during the Iraqi war. She discusses many issues that civilians may find unfamiliar and the unrelenting threats to her physical safety and mental health. Not only is there the threat of constant enemy attack, but she has to endure violence and unpredictable behaviors by other American soldiers collapsing under heavy burdens of stress. She must also face confusion in military procedures and command, working very long hours with no prior notice, and the struggle of having to lose five pounds to stay in Army regulations per physical training. Additionally, she is besieged with a sister dying in the United States and her trip home to be with her at the end as well as a later threat of serious illness in her mother. Throughout all of these harrowing stressors, Lieutenant, and then later Captain, Patrick relies on her faith in God to give her strength when she needs it most. The book is written in short, staccato bursts of events that is reminiscent of gunfire. The chapters are short which serves to ease some of the tension from unrelenting stress and there is always the comfort of her faith and scripture readings which she applies to each of her many harrowing experiences. I found her applications of scripture to the stressors she related to be applicable to stressors in a non-war and violent atmosphere in which we are out of control of events and plagued with anxiety, fear, and depression. Her coping strategies serve as a guide to the unpredictable situations in which we currently find ourselves.

Dr. Phyllis Knopp, Psychologist, Western State Hospital, Tacoma, Washington State

I enjoyed reading this book. It is a detailed account of the everyday challenges a solider faces away from home. The author shares how she handled the serious work and family issues that seemed never ending. Additionally, she created a discussion work book to further thought on facing challenges, utilizing resilience and connecting faith to overcome obstacles.

Amy Nordspearshausen, OTR/L Major Army Reserve Retired

Excellent read. Accurate description of an Occupational Therapist's role in the military during war time. The author relates how her Christian faith helped her through challenging times.

Janice Smith, OTR 1 LT US Army Retired

I love how Battle Fatigue guides people to freedom as they work through the realities of life and war. I'm grateful for all our servicemen and women, including Andrea, who go into harm's way for our freedom. This book brings empathy, hope and practical help to anyone who reads it.

Steve Harper, Associate Pastor, Grace Church, Middleburg Heights, Ohio

Battle Fatigue—Finding Your Way Back to Freedom is a story of facing the rigors of war with faith. Author Andrea Patrick served two tours of duty in Iraq and saw her share of the casualties of war from devastating injuries to death. As a lieutenant and occupational therapist in the Army Reserve, she helped soldiers overcome both the physical and mental challenges (PTSD) of war.

I enjoyed reading this authentic account of the role her personal faith in God played in helping her make sense of it all. Her faith kept her balanced, focused, provided hope, and ultimately brought her safely home after achieving the rank of Captain. The author candidly shares how "personal wars" raged at home when she was abroad with the death of her sister and the illness of her mother.

This book helped me see and feel the stress of going to war and to appreciate the strength and sacrifice of our servicemen and women. For me, it put life and death in perspective and highlighted the vital role faith plays in finding your way back to true freedom.

James C. Magruder, author of *The Glimpse,* Five time contributor to *Chicken Soup for the Soul*

With first-hand accounts, Andrea Patrick creatively and insightfully has written a book that puts readers on the path to overcoming fatigue experienced in the military and on the home front. A must read for those seeking personal wholeness and professional fulfillment.

JoAnn DePolo, artist and author of *Making it as an Artist* and contributing author of *101 Great Ways to Enhance Your Career*

BATTLE FATIGUE

FINDING YOUR WAY BACK TO FREEDOM

ANDREA A. PATRICK

WESTBOW
PRESS®
A DIVISION OF THOMAS NELSON
& ZONDERVAN

WestBow Press books may be ordered through booksellers or by contacting:

WestBow Press
A Division of Thomas Nelson & Zondervan
1663 Liberty Drive
Bloomington, IN 47403
www.westbowpress.com
844-714-3454

ISBN: 978-1-6642-5134-2 (sc)
ISBN: 978-1-6642-5133-5 (e)

Library of Congress Control Number: 2021925828

Print information available on the last page.

WestBow Press rev. date: 04/28/2022

CONTENTS

1st Deployment: Serving Others

2nd Deployment: Going Through It

INTRODUCTION

This book is for everyone who has ever wanted to 'answer the call' to serve others less fortunate. I became an Occupational Therapist to do just that. An opportunity came about to join the army reserve and use my talents and skills for a greater cause. I have a background in Psychology and I am a very dedicated born- again Christian. Was I really prepared for what I was to experience?

This account is about helping other service members, the Iraqi people, and being able to serve with exceptional professionals in a war zone. I was surrounded by environmental dangers and had to deal with major home front issues during my time in Iraq. This ordeal caused me to rely more on my faith and my relationship with God. I came to know that God IS in control and does not fail. I pray as you read this story that you too will come to know that God's grace is sufficient.

ACKNOWLEDGMENTS

The names used in this book are fictitious except for family, friends, poets, and public figures.

Thanks to all those who helped with the book: Peggi Tuscan, Jim Magruder, and Donna Ferrier.

Special thanks to my sister, Carol Hrenko, and my friends, Karen Grundy, Michaela Kekedy, and Elisa Katschka.

1ST DEPLOYMENT: SERVING OTHERS

CHAPTER 1

Election Weekend

"We are on lockdown. No one is to leave the compound. This starts right now and will continue until Monday night. All of you will stand guard duty two hours each day," the First Sergeant told us at the start of election weekend in Iraq. The Iraqis would be voting for the first time since Saddam had been driven out of power.

Most of us were quiet as we took in what we had just heard. *How did I get into this mess?* I thought. *Oh yeah. I volunteered to serve in the Army Reserve.* I was deployed with the 55th Combat Stress unit. "LT Patrick, did you check the duty roster?" CPT Hancock, the unit Chaplain, asked me as he headed out to check the roster himself.

I had met CPT Hancock in Indiana when we were training together at Ft. Harrison. The Chaplain was in his mid-thirties and had a muscular physique that resembled a superhero. In fact he had modeled a Batman costume at movie premieres. Soldiers in our unit had a nickname for him: "Pretty Boy." The Chaplain took it in stride.

Making my way toward the roster, I found out I would be on watch from 0800-1000 (8-10 a.m.) the following morning. I relayed this to the Captain. I would be lying if I didn't say I felt anxious about serving on guard duty. Up on the highest point of the roof was the lookout tower, made entirely of wood. It was 5' wide, 20' high, 10' long, and had an overhead cover. It was open so the guard could see from the tower in every direction.

Baghdad was to the north, and the forward operating bases were to the south. Our compound was situated on the perimeter of the Green Zone, which is the diplomatic area of closed streets in central Baghdad. It was called the diplomatic area because it was Saddam Hussein's place to meet visiting heads of state. Numerous armed checkpoints and "T-walls," or reinforced blast-proof concrete walls, surround this area.[1]

The compound where our unit was, near the Republican Palace in Baghdad, used to be the carriage house for Saddam Hussein's vehicles. I couldn't help but think, *I'll be a sitting duck up in that tower. I'll stick out like a sore thumb!* Just then the First Sergeant barked more orders for everyone to start placing sandbags in the doorways and along the windows. We immediately did so.

---

[1] https://en.wikipedia,org/wiki/Republican_Palace

The next briefing was at 1900 hours (7 p.m.). As we assembled for the briefing, the First Sergeant inspected each soldier's body armor, Kevlar, and rifle. "Each of you will be given extra ammo. Remember no one leaves or enters this area. Everyone knows their assignments; now get to work."

Watch time came quickly for me the next morning. I made my way up on the roof, then to the ladder that led to the lookout tower, as SGT Clement was on her way down. "Anything unusual on your watch?" I asked.

"You'll see," replied the Sergeant.

Thanks a lot. I let out a quick prayer. *Okay, Lord, please protect me.*

Once established above our compound, I could see the 14th of July Bridge, which leads into Baghdad and crosses the Tigris River. On the opposite side was the soldier statue at the traffic circle.

That day, Saturday, January 28th, was a day of action. The helicopters from the helipad across the way were cruising. When they performed their security dives, the helicopters sounded like a swarm of bees buzzing overhead. It felt as though at any time a helicopter would come crashing into the tower and onto me. Bombs were exploding and gunshots were firing all around. Smoke filled the air. I could smell the gunpowder. I kept praying our compound would not be hit. A Bible verse came to mind. "*I will never leave you nor forsake you…*" (Hebrews 13:15, NASB). Jesus said. I needed that right then!

I made sure I scanned the landscape with a full 360 sweep. Convoys of Hummers and tanks were moving along the dry, dusty desert roads. Zing! Ping! came the shots. I ducked down. I couldn't place the direction of the shots fired because of all the air traffic and constant ground noise. I felt as though I had been in the tower for an eternity that day in Iraq, but I had to stay alert and concentrate.

Just then the radio squawked and I heard, "Romeo 5, this is Foxtrot One. Romeo 5, this is Foxtrot One. Do you read, over?" It startled me and I jumped up like a frog out of a frying pan.

"Foxtrot One, this is Romeo 5. I read you loud and clear, over," I yelled into the radio.

"What's your status, over?"

"It is all clear at 1000," I reported. "This is Romeo Five over and out."

At last my watch was up. I heard a voice from below, as the Specialist who came to replace me asked, "How was your watch?"

"You'll see," I remarked with a smile, as I scrambled to get out of there.

Once I was back at headquarters, I was able to relax a bit. I let the Chaplain know how my watch had been.

The schedule at our combat stress clinic had to be kept up. I directed the daily events and classes for the soldiers entered in the program. I entered the classroom to start the Anger Management Class. Every now and then, there were explosions and shaking during class. All of us were alert and stepped into action when needed.

Each session usually lasted about an hour. The last session ended with no further interruptions.

I gathered my "battle rattle," which consisted of uniform, helmet, weighted vest, and rifle, as we left for chow at the mess hall. A group of soldiers on their way out were chatting away as we entered. One was saying, "It's too bad we can't go to the palace tonight for our weekly meeting. I'm antsy being cooped up here in this compound."

"Yea," another soldier chimed in, "I need to get my workout at the gym."

Just then the First Sergeant stepped up and roared, "What's wrong with you guys? Don't be such sissies! This lockdown is only for a few days. Now suck it up, act like soldiers, and get back to your duty stations!"

I couldn't shake the feeling that something was about to happen. After I walked into the mess hall, I retrieved my dinner. I unloaded my gear, sat with the Chaplain, and started eating. "I can feel something in the air," I told the Chaplain. "Did you ever have an intuition about something?"

The Chaplain replied, "Oh yes! I have had those incidents. I too sense something."

As the soldiers ate their meals, I couldn't help but notice tension on each of their faces. *Is it my imagination, or is some kind of danger really about to happen?* I thought. I kept my uneasiness to myself. It seemed as if everyone else was doing the same thing.

When chow time ended, I made my way back to the classroom for my next class on Conflict Resolution. As I stepped into the main classroom to get the next class underway, my reality was interrupted by a dreadful event!

CHAPTER 2

The Beginning

An explosion erupted and shook the air. It took us all by surprise. Yes, a mortar had been fired and it landed in the Republican Palace! Our compound was on alert! We awaited our orders. Everyone took battle positions. The First Sergeant called an emergency briefing. "We have been contacted to give a critical event debriefing," he said. "Two embassy workers have been killed. One was a sixty-year-old female civilian working for the Army's project and contracting office, and the other a forty-seven-year-old male Navy Lieutenant Commander. Four others were injured. The prevention team will leave at 0900 tomorrow [9 in the morning] to give the debriefing."

The forty-seven-year-old was LCDR Keith E. Taylor, from Irvine, California. He served the Commander of the U.S. Naval Forces. This was his first deployment in a hazardous environment. He had been to Haiti, and his most recent assignment had been serving in the project contracting office helping to rebuild Iraq. LCDR Taylor was also very devoted to his Christian faith. He had a wife and a new daughter who was just learning to walk. His wife regularly sent boxes of clothes, robes, and slippers for the wounded soldiers at the combat support hospital in Baghdad.[2]

According to the article, "Fallen Heroes of Operation Iraqi Freedom," LCDR Taylor had just received his orders to return to the United States. 2 ibid

The sixty-year-old woman who was killed was Barbara Heald, from Falls Church, Virginia. She had just returned to Iraq two weeks prior to her death. Barbara was an Air Force Captain in the 1970s.

---

[2] (2005, Feb. 2) Missile kills two U.S. Reconstruction workers on Election Eve in Baghdad 3/3/2005 https://www.enr.com/articles/40232-missile-kills-two-U.S.-reconstruction-workers-on-election-eve-in-baghdad-2-2-2005 (2006, Nov. 2) Fallen Heroes of Operation Iraqi Freedom. https://Fallenheroesmemorial.com/oif/profiles/taylorkeithe.html

She was in Iraq for the third time, helping rebuild the country, working as a civilian with LCDR Taylor in the project contracting office. Heald sent her sister, Geis, a picture of her in front of the crossed swords statue in Baghdad. She loved to knit, and she and her sister published a knitting magazine, according to the article, "Honoring a Woman Who Returned to Serve."[3]

Damage to Embassy roof from mortar attack

Our unit does critical event debriefings. These are meetings for those who have experienced a trauma of some sort so they can come together and converse about what happened. This can help people process the events of a tragedy and know they are not alone in their grieving and recovery process.

[3] http://www.washington post.com/wp-dyn/articles/A19952-2005Apr1. html.

The purpose and reason for our mission, however, was the Prevention Team, which is a group of soldiers who go out on assignments to teach and demonstrate self-help techniques to reduce stress. The team consists of a psychiatrist, a psychologist, a psych tech, and an occupational therapist.

I was always interested in doing challenging things. Routines bored me. So, I became an occupational therapist in 1993. I did two clinicals in order to graduate. One was in Washington State and the other in Arizona. I never married and was free to come and go as I pleased. I joined the Army Reserve after graduation so I could be an occupational therapist in the service.

Occupational therapists serve in combat stress units. I am also a devout Christian and wanted to help others. I was assigned to the 55th Combat Stress Command in Indianapolis, Indiana, even though I live in Cleveland, Ohio, and was ready to deploy and serve overseas if called to do so.

We were called up to deploy to Iraq in December 2004. This is where I met other soldiers who also served in the Reserves.

"I called to stop payment on the car insurance and cell phone," I said to my sister, Carol, as I was packing my clothes to leave for Iraq.

"I will take good care of your condo while you are away," she reassured me.

"Make sure you start my car so the battery doesn't die," I reminded her for the fourth time.

"I will," she shouted back with a stern face.

"I'm sorry, but there is so much to do to get ready. People just don't understand. I'd hate to forget something important because I will be gone a whole year."

My sister repeated, "Don't worry. I got it covered."

"I hope Nancy and Steve will be able to get along better."

"Yes," Carol agreed. It's hard to watch our sister and brother-in-law go through so much turmoil," she added.

"Make sure Mom is OK." My sister glanced at me with a look that pierced right through me. *Sisters!*

"Talk to me, please," I yelled to one of my closest friends from church later that evening. "I need to know how you feel." My friend just nodded and avoided looking at me. "I would like to know you will write and keep our friendship going while I am gone." My friend did not reply, and I had to get going. I was due to leave in two days. I prayed she wouldn't feel so bad because I was leaving. I felt bad too having to leave. Finally she did give me a hug before I left. I knew, though, God wanted me to serve in Iraq with my unit.

+ + ◆ ◆ ◆ + +

"But, Mom, I've always wanted to serve and help others," I explained at my last visit to her house before I left. "Don't worry; I will be in the safest place since they are putting me in Baghdad."

"I just don't want anything to happen to you," Mom replied. "Are you sure you will be safe?"

"The area is well guarded," I added. "It is the safest

place to be over there," yet deep inside I knew there are always dangers and no guarantees.

My mom has been through a lot. My father died from cancer when he was sixty, and my sister was going through a tough time with her husband. I kept reassuring my mom, though, because she has been on medication for anxiety and depression. She had been to the hospital after difficult times, and I did not want to put her over the edge and risk another trip.

How can I prepare for such an experience? I thought. Training always helps, but how is the emotional aspect addressed and controlled? Is it all by faith? That's what I believe. I am glad I know God and that He is with me.

I comforted my mom by telling her, "God will take care of me."

One of the residents at a facility where I was working wrote this poem for me before I left. Here is a section of it. It tells it all.

> After a short therapy spell
> Now I must say farewell
> Country and duty calls upon you
> To help others in rehab in Iraq too
> May the "Lord" give you strength
> And protect you for your duty's length[4]
> Bill Hahn, June 2004

---

[4] "Andrea Patrick". Bill Hahn, 2004

CHAPTER 3

Holiday Arrival

"I hope the rain stops," I said. "Who would have thought it would be raining in the desert?"

"I guess they have a rainy season," SGT Monroe responded.

"Yes, it is pretty miserable out there."

We had landed in Balad, Iraq, late Christmas Eve and had been bussed to an area where our tents were, right next to the airport. The First Sergeant gave each of us seven magazines with twenty rounds of ammo in each. Yes, we were on enemy soil now. I let that sink in. Eight to ten of us were assigned to one tent. We quickly learned that in Iraq the desert sand turns to a thick, grimy mud when wet, and it stuck to our boots like soft cement!

"I am so exhausted from our flight," I told the Sergeant.

"Me too," she said.

Before we knew it we were both asleep.

The next morning was Christmas and it was raining! We were able to sleep in, so when I got up I went with a battle buddy to explore the camp. I found the latrine, which was in a trailer that housed toilets; another trailer had showers. *Not so bad,* I thought.

After exploring the camp, we headed to the chow hall, which was a big tent with a cafeteria-style line. The best thing about the Army was the food! A setup of cereal and drinks were in between the tables. I went through the hot food line and saw every kind of hot breakfast food I could imagine. I had scrambled eggs, hash browns, and sausage.

We were all excited to finally be in Iraq. After the meal, we met with two 785th soldiers who were from the combat stress unit we were replacing. After they gave us a briefing about the camp and their clinic, we were free. I called my mom on a phone at the clinic.

"Mom," I said, "Merry Christmas! We landed safely, and I wanted to let you know we are safe."

It was quiet on the line for moment. Then my mom said, "You can't be my daughter; she is in Iraq. What kind of a sick joke is this?"

I said, "Mom, It's me. Don't you recognize my voice? We have special phones here in Iraq that can get through to America."

Before I knew it, she just hung up on me! I knew that my being away was stressful for her, particularly since she was on anti-depression medications. That may have been the reason she responded as she did.

I immediately called my sister, Carol, and told her to call Mom and explain. Thank God she was able to explain my phone call, and I finally got through to our mom and was able to talk to her.

A Christmas gift exchange party had started, and we made our way back to our tents. After the Chaplain spoke about Christmas, we had started exchanging gifts when the sirens went off.

"Take cover! Take cover! Incoming attack!"

We all ran out of the tents like cattle charging down a steep hill and headed for the bunkers, which were comprised of cement with sandbags all around. Each fit about fifteen people, and we were crammed! Someone started singing Jingle Bells and we all chimed in.

After what seemed like an eternity, but in fact was only about half an hour, the all clear was sounded. So, we went back to the tents and resumed our party. The Chaplain was my secret Santa; he gave me a worship CD. Later at the DFAC (dining facility) we had a wonderful Christmas dinner. I was glad I made it to Iraq safely and grateful to be with a wonderful group of soldiers, who, like myself, were ready to serve their country and, for some like me, their God.

Mortar Attack in Balad

A few days later, I was walking with a battle buddy to breakfast at the DFAC before reporting to the meeting at the 785th clinic to be trained by the combat stress team. As I approached the DFAC, I saw that no one was being allowed in, and I wondered why. So, I asked the guard at the entrance. He was telling everyone, "Do not enter; there is an unaccompanied bag out here that is being checked for a possible IED [improvised explosive device]." *Oh great,* I thought. *I wonder how long this is going to take.*

We waited and waited. Finally, the all clear was sounded, and I was able to get breakfast before reporting to the 785th. I found out later that it turned out to be someone's dirty laundry and not a bomb at all! Oh well, better to be safe!

CHAPTER 4

First Week in Baghdad

"Open this door, SPC Parks, come on!" her escort yelled, pounding on the bathroom door. After no response, CPT Rely sprang into action and busted the door down with his shoulder. He found SPC Parks standing on the toilet, attempting to hang herself with a belt from a pipe.

◆ ◆ ◆ ◆ ◆

Earlier that day…. "I am excited to teach my first class," I told CPT Rely on the morning of the first day treating clients in Iraq. CPT Rely was in charge of the clinic classes.

"Seven clients are here in the program," he informed me. "Two are suicidal. They have escorts 24/7."

"Here's my clinic schedule for them," I said as I handed it to him.

"Let's see, morning chow, workout at gym, showers clean up, classes, OT activity, evening chow, free time for phone calls, computer time. This looks good," he said.

"I'm glad I have enlisted help with the program" (there are two occupational assistants who worked with me).

"Well, I need to go. The class I am teaching on self-esteem is about to start. I'll talk to you later, Sir." My class as well as my first day went well.

Later that evening, however, I learned that SPC Parks became very upset and was crying. She had met with the psychologist earlier that day. An escort never left her side except when she used the bathroom. That's when she locked the door and tried to take her life. Thankfully, the Captain didn't hesitate to bust in and save her.

Not long afterward, SPC Parks was reassigned stateside so she could receive the psychiatric help she needed.

That incident was a sobering end to my first day of clinical work in Iraq. If I had had any doubts that our work at the clinic was critical and life-saving, SPC Parks' suicide attempt convinced me otherwise.

The clinic was located outside the Republican Palace in Baghdad. Lion statues adorned the driveway to the compound. The building had once been Saddam Hussein's carriage house with garages on the side of the property.

The stress unit that my unit was replacing converted the house into a clinic.

The first two weeks after our arrival we underwent training to understand the procedures of the clinic. Upon entering the front door, a check-in desk stood to the right with a rifle rack behind it. Each time I entered the clinic, I was required to sign in and lock up my rifle. To my left was a classroom. The computer room and a meeting room were farther down the hall. The kitchen was in the back of the building and was equipped with a stove, a large table, and a refrigerator. Adjacent to the kitchen was a storage room with a freezer. Upstairs, above the kitchen, sat three bedrooms for the enlisted staff. Back on the main floor were two rooms that held eight client bunks each, a men's bay and a women's bay. The officers slept in dormitory-style rooms converted from the garages that housed the carriages.

Soldiers were assessed at the clinic. They entered the program for three days to receive treatment and self-help classes. The most popular classes were conflict resolution, home front issues, and stress management. Challenging situations existed. Some soldiers with mental health issues responded well to treatment. Others had behavioral issues. This is why the military provides professional counselors and staff.

So began my first week of serving at the clinic. *It is going to be an interesting year!*

CHAPTER 5

Soldier Stories

Specialist Smith

"Hey guys, do we have to go out again so soon? I'm so tired I could sleep for a whole month," said SPC Smith.

"You heard the Lieutenant. Our mission is convoy ops, and we have to obey orders!" SGT Morgan replied.

The five soldiers made their way to the Humvee. SPC Smith climbed through the backseat and up into the gunnery hatch. SGT Morgan yelled out, "Let's make this a good run tonight; I'm counting on all of you to do your part!"

The route was familiar as they had been patrolling this

stretch for some time. SPC Conway performed the radio check and they were on their way. SPC Smith held onto his .50 caliber machinegun tightly. He knew the darkness could play tricks on him. They passed dark sections in neighborhoods, which at times were lit up with neon lights revealing driveways and back alleys. They were in a convoy of three vehicles.

"How are you holding up back there?" SPC Conway cried out to the soldiers in the rear. They had to stay vigilant with their M16 rifles pointing out the side windows. "As great as can be expected," replied one of the soldiers from the back of the Humvee.

SPC Smith was tired and anxious. *I hope I can make it tonight,* he thought. Sleep was creeping in, and his eyes felt like lead balloons. Just then the convoy started to speed up. The Humvee started swaying back and forth down the road, jerking SPC Smith back and forth in the gunnery hatch. "Hey! What gives?" he cried out. *This isn't right. Something's wrong!* he thought.

At night it is difficult to see the canals filled with water along the sides of the road. One wrong swerve and a Humvee can overturn, and that's exactly what happened. Suddenly, the Humvee hit a bump, crashed over the side of the road, and went into a ravine, finally landing on its side. As the vehicle was tumbling, SPC Smith ducked to avoid getting flattened. The cab quickly filled with water, and the soldiers were instantly trapped. There was no time to even release the seatbelts.

SPC Smith made his way around the inside, trying to free his fellow soldiers but to no avail. He held his breath as long as he could, looking for a way out. The doors were made of up-armored metal, so pushing his weight against them didn't budge them. Just when all seemed hopeless, he saw a light that led him to an air pocket where he was finally able to take in some fresh air. "Ahh."

The light shone through a crack, and SPC Smith realized it was another door. He kicked at it with all his might, and finally the door opened enough for him to escape. He was free, but the other guys all died in the accident, and SPC Smith became a prisoner of his thoughts, which haunted him over and over. *If only I could have moved quicker. If only we weren't going so fast. If only we weren't so tired. None of this would have happened. It's all my fault. I tried to save them but couldn't.* "I failed them," he kept saying, as he kept remembering the soldier's creed:

I will always place the mission first.
I will never accept defeat.
I will never quit.
I will never leave a fallen comrade.[5]

Fortunately, his command sent him to our clinic so he could take our classes and we could counsel him. Part of occupational therapy is performing purposeful activity. I walked to the back of our clinic in the parking lot where our Humvees were. I had SPC Smith get in the vehicle and we reenacted the event. In the light of day he realized he could not have gotten his buddies out. It was enough that he made it out alive. The Chaplain said to him, "It

---

5 https://www.army.mil/values/soldiers.html

was an act of God that a light appeared and showed you the way out. There is purpose to this. God spared you for a reason. He wants you to live and be the best you can be for others."

Our combat stress team kept encouraging SPC Smith the whole time he was in our program. When he left us, he was on a path to recovery.

Later, in my second deployment, our unit had to go through Humvee rollover training. Each of us was strapped in and turned upside down, and we had to be able to find our way out of the Humvee. I wish we could have been trained on this a little sooner. It could have made a difference for SPC Smith.

SPC Gerard was at our clinic the same time SPC Smith was. SPC Gerard was a confident soldier in his twenties, thinly built, but came across as though he were "in charge." He was very interested in learning about leadership and had read a number of John C. Maxwell's books. He also researched the topic of leadership on the internet.

The Chaplain taught a spiritual class at the clinic so he could get to know the soldiers in our program. He said to SPC Gerard, "Here you are," as he held up a book in his hand.

"What's this?" SPC Gerard replied.

"It's a book about leadership by being an example."

"Let me see it," said SPC Gerard getting up from his seat to get the book from the Chaplain. *"More than a*

Carpenter.[6] Interesting title," SPC Gerard said. "OK. I'll check it out."

I could see SPC Gerard wanted to contribute to our self-help classes, so I approached him and said, "I have an idea if you are up for it. Could you lead a class for us on leadership and what you've learned?"

He thought about it and said, "I sure will."

The rest of the day and evening, when I saw SPC Gerard, he was preparing for the class.

We awaited our teacher the next morning in the classroom where a chalkboard on wheels was situated in front of a few chairs and a sofa. There were five to six soldiers in the class, but the number of participants varied from day to day. SPC Gerard had prepared a PowerPoint presentation, which he showed on the wall. He told us about Army values, military bearing, and the importance of leadership. His readings had obviously given him a good grasp on the subject.

Later, after he had read *More than a Carpenter*, SPC Gerard attended Sunday service along with SPC Smith. The sermon was about how to achieve true greatness: by emptying ourselves so we can be available to lead and serve others. SPC Gerard wanted to commit his life to a cause and decided he wanted to become a Christian and serve Jesus Christ. The Chaplain was thrilled. At the end of the service, the Chaplain announced that SPC Gerard was to be baptized in Saddam's pool behind the

[6] McDowell, J. (1977) *More than a Carpenter*. Wheaton, Illinois. Tyndale House.

Republican Palace that Sunday evening! I was unable to attend, but I did get pictures of the event.

Saddam's pool at the Republican Palace

At different points, I would change the classes based on a soldier's needs. I would teach a class on sleep hygiene or relaxation techniques, for example, if there were soldiers suffering from insomnia or out on missions and couldn't get much sleep.

SPC Begin told us he liked poetry, so I set up a class where each soldier could talk about what he or she thought was important and express it through a story, poem, or song. PVT Kelly talked about how Lance Armstrong had made an impact on her life. SGT Hanson shared about his father and how he had learned so much from him to prepare him for military life. SPC Begin came up with a poem about the war in Iraq. I asked him if I could show it to others in the future, and he said it is OK to do so.

Pain, Hope, in Suffering
Pain of life, turmoil never ending.
Suffering the thoughts of others,
Hope of happiness, gains and losses never ending.
Death among us all who slumber here,
--- IRAQ. Anger surrounds
Wonderment, shall peace ever be found?[7]

Music, art, woodworking, and many other art forms can help us "tell it like it is" so we can get our emotions "out there" and release stress. Art is a creative and therapeutic expression. This is why purposeful activity is part of occupational therapy. Using the creative process to get our innermost thoughts and feelings out is much better than hurting someone or damaging/destroying property. Working with our hands to create something helps us get our minds off negative things and focus on something positive. Expressing our uniqueness is the spice of life.

Each of us is influenced by the creative talents of others. This soldier's poem speaks for itself! It announces a truth and speaks loudly on its own.

National Guard Soldiers

In July and August many Army National Guard members were killed in Iraq. SGT Sanders, CPT Edwards, and some of the Alpha Company soldiers of

---

[7] "Pain, Hope, in Suffering," by SPC Begin, 2005.

Camp Striker were sitting in a circle when SGT Sanders asked, "What comes to mind when you think about your fallen comrades?"

"I am angry," a Private replied. "We were just with them last night and now they are gone, just like that. It's not fair!"

"I am frustrated with the enemy. They change tactics on us every time we go out. Just when we think we know what to expect, it changes again" a Specialist added.

"Don't get me wrong; I am fearful every time I go out, but it's my duty to go," cried another soldier.

The critical event debriefing was in progress at Camp Striker with two of our personnel from the stress unit. The National Guard soldiers were from Georgia and had been in Iraq only a few months. Four of their men had just been killed after a bomb attack on a Baghdad road.

Back at our clinic in Baghdad, I was in a meeting discussing the upcoming Moral, Wellness, and Recreation (MWR) night our unit was about to have since I was the MWR officer. "This time we will have more activities," I said. "There will be chess, spades, karaoke, Halo games, ping pong, and a pie-eating contest. The winners will each get a voucher for the PX."

SGT Douglas won the pie-eating contest. SPC Stewart won at chess. I sang a Carole King song at karaoke but SGT Lawrence won the singing event. One surprise that I count as God supplying our needs came when a co-worker Steve, sent me two boxes of comfort food, containing Hostess pies, Pringles, etc. just in time for MWR night. We had six additional soldiers that week.

Later that week, another four National Guard troops were killed from the 48th Brigade Combat team from the same platoon! This time their vehicle rolled over a bomb minutes from returning to Camp Striker. Eight soldiers were gone in a week's time! Alpha Company started with eleven soldiers; now there were only three left! This war was different from other wars. In previous wars it was easier to tell who our enemy was. Now anyone could be a suicide bomber or set off IEDs.

Six soldiers from Camp Striker came to our stress clinic one morning. One was a Lieutenant and another was an SFC (Sergeant First Class). These men knew the importance of getting counseling and having some down time. The General overseeing these soldiers made sure we helped them. All of my training and our PR campaigns about combat stress paid off. It is so important for troops to debrief and to work through Post-Traumatic Stress Disorder (PTSD).

PTSD can happen to anyone at any level. According to the Mayo Clinic, PTSD is a mental health condition triggered by experiencing or witnessing a terrifying event.[8] Symptoms may include intrusive thoughts or flashbacks of traumatic events, recurring nightmares, emotional numbness, avoidance of any reminder of the trauma, and difficulty concentrating.

I was impressed by these guys. They were quick learners

---

[8] Post Traumatic Stress Disorder (2018) *Mayo-Clinic.com* word looked up in 2018 retrieved from Mayo-Clinic https://www.mayo-clinic.org/diseases-conditions/post-traumatic-stress-disorder/symptoms-causes/syc-20355967

and wanted to take back to their troops all we had taught them. Plus, we were having our MWR, event, which meant more socializing and what I call "normalcy." One of the occupational therapy goals was social interaction and participation, which helped reintegrate a person back to a regular pre-war routine. Work, rest, and play were the daily living activities and needed to be maintained in balance. Too much of any one of these would throw off even the most disciplined Marine. Especially during war time, a balance in these areas helped us keep mentally fit.

Sad news continued with more deaths that week. Fourteen soldiers from the Marine Reserve Unit Lima Company were killed in Hathida forty miles northwest of Baghdad. Six were from my home state of Ohio. They were from the 3rd Battalion, 25th Marine Regiment, 4th Marine Division based out of Brook Park, Ohio. Others were from Columbus; Seven Hills; Willoughby; and my hometown, Parma. The President gave a speech about the tragedy, and there was a memorial service that very week back home. I would have attended if I had been there. Instead I was privileged to serve six other National Guard soldiers from Georgia. In reality they served me.

The Chaplain and two other staff members went to Camp Striker for two weeks after these soldiers came to our clinic to assist the remaining soldiers at Camp Striker with the grieving process and conduct post-trauma classes.

In-Clinic Soldier Stories

Midway into our deployment, I was acting OIC (Officer in Charge) of the clinic, since CPT Barley was on R&R (rest and relaxation). I was told to make sure things stayed calm and in order while he was away.

We had one client who was depressed and two others who were suicidal. SGT Cramer, the (Nov 3) Army specialty for Certified Occupational Therapy Assistant (COTA), was on duty with the clients that night, and I was staying around the clinic to make sure things were going well.

It was getting late and I said to the staff, "I am going to my room. If you need me, let me know."

Later, I heard a knock at my door. SGT Peterson, one of the psych aides, was standing in the hall.

"What is going on?" I asked.

She replied, "One of the clients attempted to mutilate herself. I caught her with a plastic knife from the kitchen, and she was trying to cut her arms. She was going to carve her son's name on her arm. I stopped her before she could do it."

SGT Peterson filled me in on the background of the client. It seems that because the client had to come to our clinic, she was not able to go home on R&R. She was upset about this and texted her son at home. He was so angry that he called her a liar. This was too much for the client to bear, so she started to act out and grabbed the knife from the kitchen. This was when SGT Peterson found and stopped her.

"Where was her escort?" I asked.

"I don't know," replied SGT Peterson. "The incident happened so fast. I haven't seen the escort."

I was relieved that this incident did not go further, but I still had to write an incident report. Since this was a behavioral issue of harming oneself or others, protocol was to evacuate the client back to the States. The only problem was this client's unit was taking a long time to get the necessary paperwork for her to go. The unit was due at the clinic the next morning for an update with this client.

The next day we awaited the client's unit. They came and were ready to meet with her. She and her escort came to the meeting, but before we could settle in and close the door, the client ran out the back door by the kitchen. It was a FREE FOR ALL; we all scattered to find her.

It so happened at this time that SGT Daniels, our social worker and our unit psychiatrist, Major Black, were returning from a mission and walking back to the clinic. The client ran right past them in a wild frenzy! They quickly subdued her and brought her back inside the clinic. She was screaming, yelling, and squirming. Her unit commander wanted us to keep her at the clinic until the proper paperwork would be ready. So we waited.

Later that evening, the XO (Executive Officer) of our unit and the client had a shouting match. I heard furniture being thrown around. The client had thrown a container of orange juice at the XO, and the staff came running and got the situation under control. Finally we received the proper paperwork, took the client to the CSH, and she was on her way to Germany for psychiatric screening.

CHAPTER 6

Mission Intensifies

"It's time to go," Major Black said. I followed him to the Humvee.

"How can I assist you today?" I asked.

"When we get to the memorial service I want you to be available in case anyone needs our services. Be ready to tell them about our clinic and mission." A Colonel had committed suicide by using his own pistol. He was going home soon, so it was unexpected.

"What job did this Colonel do at the Palace?" I asked the Major.

Major Black said he was serving with the Multinational Security Transition Command. His duty was to oversee the training of Iraqis for civilian police duty with a private military company.

> But sources say in May 2005 someone sent COL Westhusing an anonymous letter indicating abuse of power and fraud. According to Wikipedia, there were allegations about inadequate competence of trainers; false resumes; and disappearance of weapons, radios, and equipment. Employees even boasted of killing Iraqis.
>
> COL Westhusing wanted to expose these injustices. He was so torn apart that he was planning to inform General Petraeus of his resignation. Michelle Westhusing, the Colonel's wife, mentioned in an article from the "Sworn Statement [of Michelle Westhusing]" that COL Westhusing, who was left-handed, was found in his trailer with a gunshot wound behind his left ear from his own 9mm Beretta service pistol on June 5, 2005, a month and three days before his tour of duty was to end.[9]

He had informed General Petraeus about these issues early that same morning. His suicide note was published in the *Texas Observer* on March 8, 2007. It read:

---

[9] Theodore S. Westhusing, 2018, in *Wikipedia.com* looked up in 2018 from https://en:wikipedia.org/wiki/theodore_s._westhusing

Thanks for telling me it was a good day until I briefed you. You are only interested in your career and provide no support to your staff—no mission support, and you don't care. I cannot support a mission that leads to corruption, human rights abuse, and liars. I am sullied—no more. I didn't volunteer to support corrupt, money-grubbing contractors, nor work or commanders only interested in themselves. I came to serve honorably and feel dishonored. I trust no Iraqi. I cannot live this way. All my love to my family, my wife, and my precious children. I love you and trust you only. Death before being dishonored anymore. Trust is essential—I don't know who to trust anymore. Why serve when you cannot accomplish the mission, when you no longer believe in the cause, when your every effort and breath to succeed meets with lies, lack of support, and selfishness? No more. Reevaluate yourselves, commanders. You are not what you think you are and you know it.

COL Ted Westhusing

Life needs trust. Trust is no more in Iraq.[10]

---

[10] Bryce, Robert. (2007, March 9) I am sullied no more. *Texas Observer.* https://www.texasobserver.org12440-1-am-sullied-no-more-faced-with-iraq-corruption-col.ted-westhusing-chose-death-before-dishonor

The *New York Times/Los Angeles Times* reporter, T. Christian Miller, reported on the possibility that he was murdered by defense contractors who feared he would become a whistle-blower against their alleged fraudulent activity throughout the Iraq War. 9 ibid

Westhusing's funeral service and burial at West Point were attended by General Peraeus (who returned from Iraq for the event) as well as three other Generals of two stars or more.

The controversy of Westhusing's death is depicted in the one-act play "Duty, Honor, Profit," written by Westhusing's West Point classmate, Dave Tucker, a Seattle playwright.

We were at the memorial service held in Iraq, and Major Black, who is a psychiatrist, was there in case anyone needed to talk or debrief. After words were said at the service, Major Black told the people in attendance about our clinic right outside the Palace area, so that if anyone needing the services of our unit, he and I would be available to help.

Mission Intensifies 2

March 9, 2005

I felt the ground shake. An explosion erupted! Black smoke filled the air. I was finishing my morning jog along the compound when suddenly I heard the PA announcement, "Take cover, take cover, go to bunkers, go to bunkers!" I ran as fast as I could back to the clinic. "There is a PA warning going off," I shouted.

The Captain yelled, "Yes, I heard it! Be ready for a lockdown. Take roll call. Have the team report to the conference room now!"

Later at the briefing, CPT Brenning said, "The bombings this morning involved a garbage truck that ran through a check point. The Marines had no choice but to fire upon the truck. The two drivers in it were killed. The explosion was the IED inside the truck. Twenty-seven people were injured. Contract workers were among them. The 86th CSH will need some help today. The Al-Sadir Hotel is now off limits for our unit."

I thought to myself, *Is this really happening? It's so close! Our team had been to the Al-Sadir hotel a few times to eat at the dining facility there. Now it's off limits.*

"The prevention team will visit the 86th CSH tomorrow to provide services to the contract workers and hospital staff," the Captain informed us. "The restoration team [which I was part of] is to continue their program and classes at the clinic."

According to an article in the *China Daily*,

> Wednesday's massive dawn blast in central Baghdad shook nearby buildings, injured dozens of people, and covered a huge swath of sky with acrid black smoke. Police said a group of insurgents wearing police uniforms shot a guard dead at the Agriculture Ministry's gate, allowing the truck to enter a compound the ministry shares with the adjacent Al-Sadir Hotel.

Guards in the area then fired on the vehicle, trying to disable it before it exploded. Ibn-Nasif Hospital, counted twenty-seven wounded. Another hospital, the Al-Kind, had at least three dead and eight wounded. The truck blew up in a parking lot, damaging twenty cars.[11]

Our hospital in the Green Zone, with the 86th CSH, would get some of these casualties too.

Here is a picture of the Ibn-Sina hospital in the Green Zone in Baghdad.

Ibn-Sina Hospital

---

[11] (2005, March 09) Suicide truck Bomb kills three in Baghdad. https://www.chinadaily.com,cn/english/doc/2005-03-09/content.423394.html

The Serious Side of Our Mission 1

When I considered why some who wish to serve die early and others don't want to serve but want to end their lives, I realized it is two sides of the same coin.

"Hurry up; let's get her inside." One night in April after most of us had gone to bed, a Humvee pulled into our compound. Three soldiers lifted another soldier into the clinic. "We need help here!" Two of our Medic EMS-trained soldiers were awakened and came to assist.

"This is the Combat Support Hospital, isn't it?" It was dark because it was late at night, and the convoy thought they were at the 86th CSH. Plus, the name of our compound could be mistaken being called a medical company, "55th Medical Company Combat Stress Control."

"Help us! Quick! We were hit by an IED and PVT Huff was driving!" Huff's legs were severed by the blast. The medics in our company did everything they could, but she bled to death from the wounds. She was taken to the 86th CSH.

Sam (short for Samantha) Huff joined the Army at age sixteen. She was from Tucson, Arizona, and played the drums in the marching band. She was a member of the 170th Military Police Company, 504th Military Battalion, 42nd Military Police Brigade, based at Fort Lewis, Washington. Her father is a retired Tucson police officer and now plays guitar in a band. Her mother had served in the Marine Corps in Vietnam. PVT Huff wanted to pursue a degree in psychology and then go to work for the FBI.

PVT Sam Huff was not able to handle the turret gun in the Humvee, so she did the driving. Her convoy patrolled Route Irish Road (between the airport and Baghdad), a very dangerous route.

PVT Huff's last words were to her Sergeant: "Tell my mom I love her, and tell my dad good luck on his album" according to a Department of Defense news release.[12] PVT Sam Huff received the Purple Heart, Bronze Star, and Good Conduct Medal. She was buried with full military honors at Arlington National Cemetery.

I may not understand these things now, but I will in eternity. God is faithful to His word and He is sovereign. He is in control of all things. Isaiah 14:24 (ESV) says, "The LORD of hosts has sworn: "As I have planned, so shall it be, and as I have purposed, so shall it stand," and Isaiah 55:8-9 (NASB) says, "For My thoughts are not your thoughts, Nor are your ways My ways,' declares the LORD. 'For *as* the heavens are higher than the earth, So are My ways higher than your ways And My thoughts than your thoughts." I believe His word.

---

[12] (2005, April 19) News Release from United States Department of Defense, Arlington cemetery,net/smhuff.htm

CHAPTER 7

Humanitarian Missions

"Chaplain!" I called out. "What time are we going?"

"We are to meet at the hospital around 1300," he replied.

"I can't wait to go and see the families at the apartments." This was the day of our first humanitarian mission with the 86th CSH (Combat Support Hospital). "I have some candy and cookies to hand out," I said to him.

The Chaplain and Commander prayed together before we left in a convoy. The first and last vehicles had the gun turrets. The 86th CSH had collected candy, coloring books, school supplies, and toys. We arrived at an apartment complex to a group of women and children waiting for us. They surrounded our vehicles as we pulled in and greeted us with smiles and hugs.

"This complex was hit with a rocket two weeks ago," our guide said. "It hit the top part of the building over there," he continued as he pointed at one of the rooftops. "Some of the people here are squatters and the government may soon come and kick them out." Nevertheless there was a large group of women and children waiting for us.

It was such a joy to see the children and the expressions on their faces. I handed out pens, paper, and the candies I had brought. The children pulled the pens out of my hands so fast they were gone before I knew it. Songs were sung and games were played as we entertained the little ones, who were so taken with the soldiers.

One girl would not let go of my hand. She wanted to be in pictures with the soldiers. The women were very thankful that we had come.

"Hurry up; we need to get going so we can visit the school," our guide announced. As we left I will never forget the time we had and how welcome we were.

We headed to a high school where girls attended classes in the mornings and boys attended in the afternoon. Some teachers let us in to a courtyard outside the building where we unloaded boxes filled with school supplies and backpacks from the trucks and Humvees. It was around 110 degrees, and I was in full battle gear, so I could feel the perspiration on my forehead and face. It didn't matter, though, because it was a great day. The experience of helping others was all I needed. It was a pleasant reward.

Standing with Girl

Boy admiring rifle

Michael W. Smith's new CD had been released before our unit deployed. There was a song on that CD that had to do with helping others that touched me deeply.

A silent cry from a distant land
Crying for a helping hand
How long will it go on?
Ignorance and vanity
Supercedes humanity, so

How long will it go on? It was called, "We Can't Wait Any Longer."[13] A part of the song is in Swahili. The children are crying out for someone to save them. It 'struck a nerve' in me. It related to the Iraqi people, and our military stepping in willing to help.

This is how the Iraqi people must have felt because Saddam Hussein was in power. I was thankful just to have been part of this trip and to be able to bring some love and gifts to the people there.

Humanitarian Missions 2

"We are going to put these shoes we received in European sizing order," I told the clients after class at the clinic one day.

"This is going to take a while," a client replied.

"Yes, I know, but with all of us doing this together, it should go faster. The Chaplain is going to help us too."

In July, the second humanitarian mission with the 86th CSH was only a few days away. The Chaplain and I had written to our churches back home and asked them to send shoes. And boy, did they. We received three hundred pairs.

"OK," the Chaplain said, "let's put the children's sizes here in these boxes with the sizes labeled and the adult sizes here." It took us three hours to put all the shoes in the correct size boxes.

---

[13] Smith, Michael W. (2004) We can't wait any longer. https"// genius.com/Michael-w-smith-we-can't-wait-any-longer-lyrics.

"Now they are ready for the mission tomorrow," the Chaplain said.

"I am ready," I said the next morning to the Chaplain.

On our way to the CSH later, two bomb blasts went off. We met at the hospital for the mission. Just as we were pulling in to the hospital parking lot, we heard the hum of helicopter blades.

"Incoming helicopters!" shouted one of the doctors at the CSH. Two soldiers came in on cots to the hospital. One had a major facial injury, and the other had a right lower extremity injury from an IED. The hospital Chaplain was coming to the humanitarian mission with us, but he had to speak and pray with the injured soldiers first.

We left a little later and came to a school. This time we had a line waiting for us in front of the playground. Our interpreter said, "We need to keep this organized, so we will open and shut the gates of the playground and only let in a few people in at a time to try on shoes and take the ones they want. Then we will have them leave and bring in a few more people." This turned out to be a good plan, but the people wanted to stay longer and take more than one pair. The children were everywhere. We had to try to keep things in order.

"Ma'am, stop taking so many," one of the soldiers urged. The interpreter was called to the area where the women were trying to take too many shoes. The interpreter started speaking louder and louder, and the lady in charge of the school wanted more school supplies.

We helped some maintenance workers from the school get the sizes they needed. They were smiling from ear to ear when they got their new shoes. I had them pose for a picture.

A little later the scene calmed down and we were able to leave. Below are a few pictures from the mission that day.

Men with shoes

Women finding shoes

When people don't have much, they are so grateful, humble, and willing to receive the "little things." Watching the joy on their faces during the visit reminded me to be thankful and not think too "highly of myself," as the word of God says. After all, I am one of God's creations.

A Beatitude came to my mind, Matthew 5:5: "Blessed are the meek: for they shall inherit the earth" (KJV). In other words, blessed (happy) are those who are meek (gentle), for they will inherit the earth (inherit the land and enjoy peace and prosperity). A person who is meek has joy. This is the kind of spirit I noticed on their faces.

CHAPTER 8

Hospital Work

"CPT Douglas!" I called out. "Can I assist the orthotist with the incoming wounded?" CPT Douglas was the physical therapist at the 86th CSH. I worked with him every week on my day off from the clinic. A mass casualty was going on! This was Saddam's private hospital for himself, his family, and the Baath party prior to the Iraqi war. The Ibn Sina hospital, as it was called, was in the Green Zone in Baghdad. The U.S. Army saw three hundred trauma cases a month between 2003 and 2009. A DVD called "Baghdad ER" was filmed there about the 86th CSH.

"Go ahead," he said. I walked to the lobby where the

hospital staff were bringing in Iraqi wounded from a mass casualty. I could feel the rush in the air. It was like a well-organized orchestra. There was rhythm to the movement as staff members were lining up victims for triage. Most were Iraqi men being brought in from the helicopter pad outside. I had heard they were expecting a total of twelve injured. I jumped in and helped bring the wounded into the room we used as an ER.   A doctor shouted out, "Move that stretcher here!" "Get that one over by the wall. He will need surgery soon," a nurse ordered.

"What happened to you?" I asked as I helped a young Iraqi man get off the stretcher and onto a chair.

"I was in a car and a suicide bomber got in. He blew us all up!" The man had a helmet and flack vest on at the time. "I now have a bad headache and I can't breathe right." I noticed both of his forearms were in ace wraps.

"He may have fractured the left wrist," the orthotist, SGT Gonzales, said to me.

The man exclaimed, "I was unconscious for a while and I woke up here!"

I had to leave him to go with SGT Gonzales to help splint a man who had a fractured knee and shrapnel in his lower leg. As I was putting on my gloves, I noticed that there were many casualties that filled the ER that day.

"Ohhh," the man with the fractured knee cried out in pain. Then SGT Gonzales told me, "Hold the leg still now, LT Patrick, while I get the plaster around his leg." This man also had a fractured jaw and a bullet in his lung. After we splinted his leg, he was on his way to surgery.

In the ER I observed a man with a gash in his gastric

muscle. I could see clear to the muscle level. One of the hospital staff told me, "It is kept open like this; then skin is grafted onto it."

I assisted the Sergeant with another leg splint. "We will be taking him to surgery now. I can use your help there if you want to come."

"You bet," I told the Sergeant.

"LT Patrick," I heard my name called. It was CPT Douglas who found me in the ER. "I need your help back in therapy."

"I am on my way," I said, a little disappointed not to be able to help in surgery.

Another time at the hospital I was able to help an Iraqi Army Colonel who had scars and pins in his arm as a result of a gunshot wound. He was limited in movement, so I gave him ten exercises to do, and I would see him again in two weeks.

I saw an Iraqi child who had been burned by an IED. She needed to start using her hands even though they were painful and wounded. So, I sat down with her and we did some coloring, writing, and playing with a ball.

"Hold still," I told a Specialist while fitting a splint for his hand and wrist. SPC Johnson had been in an IED explosion, and shrapnel had hit his forearm and went up to his neck.

"We were going only three miles per hour, and I knew something was about to go down," exclaimed the Specialist. "I was up in the turret and I saw a light flash. I knew it was a signal because all of a sudden an explosion occurred and I got injured."

I explained to the Specialist, "I see you have stitches in the forearm here, and the ulnar nerve is injured. That's why you can't extend your fingers. This splint will protect your wrist, hand, and fingers. Wear it during the day."

"I am going to Germany for surgery," SPC Johnson told me.

"Good," I replied. "You will get therapy there after surgery. You will do well."

◆◆◆◆◆◆

I saw a woman who had fractured her hand while visiting Egypt. Her husband was on the election board in Iraq. "I want to thank you for taking care of me in therapy," she told me. "I would like you to come to my house for a party."

I replied, "Thank you. I will do my best to attend." We had learned it would be a dishonor not to go to a social event given by the Iraqi people. They are very family oriented and social. It is considered an honor if they invite you to their home.

I talked with my commander and she told me it would be all right to go with a battle buddy. CPT Sullivan, a social worker, and I went together. Our Humvee had a formal escort to the neighborhood, which was in the Green Zone. The Green Zone is the diplomatic area in central Bagdad protected by T-walls and the home to a few Army forward operating bases.

"It is weird following an escort," I said to CPT Sullivan.

"Yes, it is," he replied.

We headed down side streets and around corners protected by high fences. Once we parked in the driveway of a moderate-size house, and we were joined by armed contract workers who walked us into the entrance. I counted eight guards in the front yard alone.

Wow, I feel like I am in one of those mafia movies. What have I gotten myself into?

Upon entering the house, we were greeted by the patient, her daughter, and her spouse.

I could see a nice, but small, home. At table with all kinds of well-prepared foods on it was set in the living room. There was a mixture of U.S. and British soldiers, embassy workers, and friends of the family at this party.

"Welcome, so glad you could come," said our hostess. As the party progressed, I was privileged to converse about the future elections. The New Constitution for the Iraqis had just been written. The spouse of my patient was on the board of elections in Iraq!

When it was time to go, we headed back in our Humvee. "What? No escort home?" I asked CPT Sullivan.

"I guess not," he replied.

It was pitch black out. We ambled along quietly and slowly, feeling a little like an orange cat sitting in the middle of the road standing out for all to see. We sort of spooked each other when we saw some Iraqis that noticed our Humvee. We never knew what might have happened while we were there, so we were not taking any chances. Once out of the neighborhood, we floored it back to our compound as fast as we could!

CHAPTER 9

Sniper

"Are you ready to go to the gym?" SGT Mitchell yelled to SPC Walker.

"So ready!" the Specialist replied, putting on his Kevlar (army helmet) and flack vest. "After that shift today, I need a workout."

They made their way into the street and along the dusty sidewalks. The hot, dry air hit their faces like a hot hair blower blast. They came to the turn in the street that led to the gym. Baam! SPC Walker felt an intense pressure hit him square in the forehead. He dropped to the ground with a thud!

"What in the world?" Terror struck his face.

He heard SGT Mitchell yell, "Get down! Someone's firing at us." Both soldiers low crawled behind a vehicle on the street. After some time both made their way into a nearby building. They reported to the guard at the desk that there was small arms fire going on.

The guard received information that a sniper had recently been firing on soldiers in the Green Zone.

'Wow!" exclaimed SPC McBride, looking at a dent in his Kevlar. If it weren't for my Kevlar, I'd be a goner."

At our morning meeting that week, the First Sergeant said, "We need to be aware of snipers around the hospital. Make sure to take every precaution when out, especially when going to the hospital, gym, or Sunday services."

I started thinking about the danger of being shot by a sniper. No matter where I was, anything could happen at any time. Accidents or trauma could occur anywhere. So were the odds higher when I was in Iraq than when I was in the States? Who is in charge of my life anyway? As a Christian I believe God is. Isaiah 49:16 says, "…Behold, I have inscribed you on the palms *of My hands…*" (NASB). I am in the palm of His hand. He created me in the first place. I can trust and rest in Him. Faith comes down to one thing: do I really trust Him?

CHAPTER 10

Working with the Chaplain

"Wait for me!" I cried out to Chaplain Hancock. We were on our way to the Wednesday Bible study with some of the 86th CSH soldiers and had to drive from our compound to the building across from the hospital.

The Chaplain had his own vehicle. Chaplains are not allowed to carry weapons. So, I was teased a lot about riding "shotgun" for him because I had a rifle.

"I am ready now," I said climbing into the passenger side of the vehicle.

"What is the new Bible study about?"

"The title is, 'Getting Out of the Boat,' the Chaplain replied. It is a study about having faith and believing God."

As we arrived I noticed two Iraqi women. I walked to where they were and said, "Hi, welcome." I learned they were both Christians. Not everyone in Iraq is Muslim. Some Iraqis are Catholic, though I did not know if this was the case with them because we had to start the study and I did not have the opportunity to ask them.

The study went well, and afterward one of the women spoke to us. "The times have been hard here," she said. "I asked Jesus for a sign of His presence. I live with my father, who is Muslim, and my mother, who is a Christian. One day I saw the tree in my yard was dead. I prayed about it. All of a sudden it started to produce fruit! I ran to my parents and told them. We all ate fruit from this tree that was dead before and is alive now! I believe this is a sign from God. I am excited to come to this Bible study."

My friend, JoAnn, sent me a care package. In it were two cross pins to give to somebody. The two Iraqi women came to mind. The next week at the Bible study I gave each of them a cross. I really believe God wanted them to have them, and my friend sent them at just the right time.

⁘

"I received a care package today," shared one of the nurses at our Sunday service one morning. "I was sent a new Bible. I already have two Bibles, so I prayed about what to do with it. The night we received those twenty-seven casualties from the garbage truck IED, I was working. One of the contractor workers was my patient. He asked me for a Bible. I remembered I had just gotten the new one from the care package and I gave it to him! Praise God He answers prayers."

"We have to give a critical event debriefing," said LTC Myers. SGT Davidson and Major Hanson got ready to go. The Specialist behind the desk opened the rifle rack so each soldier could retrieve their firearms. They went to the parking lot behind the clinic and entered the Humvee assigned to the prevention team.

"Hope we can help these soldiers," MAJ Hanson said.

"Remember to let them do the talking," LTC Meyers chimed in.

"Yes, that's right; it is better that way," SGT Davidson said smiling. Then we don't have to talk as much."

They crossed the traffic circle where the soldiers' statue stood and drove through the arches (depicting the entrance to Saddam's embassy buildings).

Bam! Crash! A loud explosion rocked the Humvee.

"What was that?" LTC Myers cried out.

"I think a mortar hit," said SGT Davidson. The Humvee was stopped in traffic.

"It looks like there is nowhere to go for now," MAJ Hanson declared.

After sitting still awhile, an MP made his way to the Humvee. "You need to turn around and head back," he instructed. "No one is allowed to go further on this road."

"OK," the Lieutenant Colonel answered.

The team made its way back to the clinic. When they returned and told us what had happened, I said, "My friend at church along with the prayer team, felt led to pray for our unit this morning and with the time difference it was about the time you were out".

"Wow, we are so glad for that," said SGT Davidson. "Thank them for us."

"I will," I replied. I made sure I sent an email to my friend Michaela to thank them.

CHAPTER 11

Lessons Learned

It really wasn't that different serving in Iraq than it was working at home in the States. I worked in the clinic with clients in Iraq, and I worked with patients in the hospital at home. People are people whether they are soldiers or civilians. Yes, situational awareness was needed more in Iraq since that was a war zone and the risks were higher, but anything can happen at home too. It may be calmer at home, but the potential for chaos and the unexpected exists anywhere.

Since I returned home, the United States has become even more dangerous. More suicide bombings and terrorist attacks have been occurring, sad to say. Lawlessness contributes to this, which leads to these disasters.

Working with the Army is a 24/7 job. I had my shift time in Iraq as well as my down time. I needed to be ready to go back to work at any time if things changed, though, and they could change very quickly.

Stress was more intense in the war zone, which contributes to battle fatigue, a mental illness caused by fighting in a way that causes extreme feelings of nervousness and depression, according to the Merriam-Webster dictionary. Working with difficult clients or patients is stressful no matter where you are.

When I first came to Iraq, the adrenalin was high. I noticed everything around me. I was vigilant. After a time, this lessened and I became more acclimated to the environment. At first I was afraid of my own shadow, so to speak. While vigilance is needed, after a time it can lead to exhaustion. Letting my guard down completely, however, would have been careless in a hazardous zone.

Working with military staff was like working with coworkers at home. The big difference was I was a trained soldier and able to defend myself with a weapon if need be. I worked with young and inexperienced soldiers and new health care workers. They had been trained, but working with staff and clients would prove how good their training was. The beginning was rough because discipline and more training were needed. After time, however, these young soldiers learned quickly and were able to work well with the clients.

The stress affected everyone. Longer hours, being away

from home, home-front issues, and unexpected events on the war front took their toll. Our unit was knowledgeable about this, though, because this was our area of expertise. Some in my unit ended up with compassion fatigue, which, according to Merriam-Webster, is physical and mental exhaustion and emotional withdrawal experienced by those who care for sick or traumatized people over an extended period of time.[14] Balance is needed when dealing with stress. Stress management and knowing how to de-stress are so important. We had two sayings overseas: "It is what it is" and "What can they do to me? Send me to Iraq."

It can get "crazy," excuse the pun, working with the same people day after day. Getting on each other's nerves does happen. I am an advocate of work, rest, and play. So rest and relaxation, "R&R," is so important. A good commander knows this and sees that the troops get it. Our commanders did this and I am glad.

The soldiers I served were going through so many changes so fast. They were on the front lines and going on patrol runs in dangerous areas on a daily basis. If a soldier has poor coping skills to begin with, he or she is asking for trouble.

This is why the clinic trains the clients on basic life skills. We taught classes on home-front issues, anger and stress management, conflict resolution, relaxation

---

[14] Compassion fatigue (2018) in *Merriam-Webster.com* word looked up in 2018 retrieved from https://www.merriam-webster.com/dictionary.html

techniques, sleep hygiene, how thoughts affect you, and spiritual health.

Everyone is made up of a mind, soul, body, and spirit. So training in all areas is important. I endorsed the spiritual health classes, which taught a holistic approach to mental, spiritual, and physical health.

After serving the year in Iraq, the return home had some effects too. Cars on the sides of the roads suddenly bothered me. I thought they would just blow up. I could not look at them and instead kept my focus in front of me when I drove by them. I would also find things that looked suspicious around me and avoid them. When there was a thunderstorm I would put on my Kevlar and hide in the crawlspace under the steps. I could not watch violent movies for a while. I also did not like people complaining about trivial things, because only the life-and-death things mattered.

After obeying orders for a year away, I found I had become intolerant of certain authority figures because I was now out and free and did not want to obey them. I wanted control back. It took a while to readjust to these things.

The first deployment focused on serving others. It was a fulfilling time of doing occupational therapy, teaching, playing on the worship team at church, working with the Chaplain, and inventing a stress-management game that helped the soldiers learn self-help skills. Other areas of services included treating hand and arm injuries at the combat support hospital; being Morale, Recreation, and

Welfare officer for my unit; and going on humanitarian missions.

My second deployment would be completely different! I didn't know it then, but I'd be "going through it" (experiencing difficult and challenging times) myself in my next tour to Iraq.

2ND DEPLOYMENT: GOING THROUGH IT

CHAPTER 12

Preparing To Go

"CPT Patrick!" the Commander called out my name. "You may have to be refradded!"

Refradded means not being able to deploy because of a medical issue. I knew others who had trained hard with us only to be sent back because of hearing, vision, or back problems.

Getting called back to Iraq for the second time was not as thrilling as the first. The timing could not have been worse. My sister was fighting colon cancer at age fifty-one. I had just gotten resettled in my job from the last deployment and didn't want to uproot again. It takes energy to take up and move out. Once again, I had to get my house in order, put stop payments on bills, and do more paperwork. Plus, my unit had to go through SRP, clearing medical in order to be eligible to deploy. Then there is training all over again! So, to say the least, I wasn't as excited as I was the first time. I had been promoted to Captain now too.

I met a new group of professional reserve soldiers, and the training this time, which included firing some heavy rounds at Ft. Dix, was a little more extensive. All in all, we made it through the scenarios and exercises.

I was assigned to be in charge of the Restoration Team in Balad. It was one of the largest military bases in Iraq until withdrawal in 2011. According to Wikipedia, it was formerly the largest Iraqi Air Force base during the Saddam Hussein era.

I was to serve with the soldiers who were formerly deployed. This made it a lot easier for me, and I was glad.

Ft. Hood was our last stop before we were validated to go.

"It seems your urine test came back positive for pregnancy!" If it wasn't for the seriousness of this predicament I would have laughed. Everyone could see that I was not a spring chicken anymore, as I was approaching fifty.

"There has to be some sort of mix-up," I said. "Why would *I* test positive?" I knew menopause had hit. The staff at medical were ruthless. I had to wait to be retested again after taking some medication to make sure I was not pregnant. By now, after all the training and unit cohesion, everything within me wanted to go. Serving together with a unit of medical professionals was the best part, especially after all the training we had been through. It was an honor to be called to go and represent the best country on earth.

I called a friend at work and told her about my predicament. Instead of consoling me she started laughing and said, "I guess you are trying to get out of going to Iraq by shacking up with Mitch" (a fellow coworker). This did not set right with me. I immediately got angry and hung up on her, though I did call back and apologize later.

CHAPTER 13

OT visit: Camp Liberty

After getting settled in Balad, my team commander informed me, "COL Branson wants you to go to Camp Liberty in Baghdad to check up on the clinic there." The Commander wanted me to give some insights and suggestions about the clinic setup.

I said, "OK, when do I go?"

"As soon as we get you on the manifest roster." I really was not too excited to go. I was content to stay. The soldiers there were all new and on their first deployment, including MAJ Franklin, the occupational therapist in charge of the restoration team there. She was in her mid-forties and had reddish hair and a spunky personality.

So I got my gear together and reported at "zero dark thirty" in full battle rattle. Our team Commander drove me to the airport, and I was able to get out on a C130.

SPC Diamond picked me up at Camp Liberty. "Good to see you, Specialist," I said. We had trained together, so we were good friends by now and were able to enjoy some down time. We went for some coffee and then to the flea market where I picked up some DVDs. The Iraqis copy them and I bought them cheap.

Then I went to MAJ Franklin's "Chu" (contained handling unit). It's a small trailer where I settled in for a little while. The Major was at the clinic. I went there later, was introduced to the staff, had a tour of the clinic, and was able to see how it was set up. I met the psychiatrist I had trained with, MAJ Housel. He had joined us in Kuwait before we went to Balad. I also met LCDR Springle, a social worker from the Navy.

"How do you like serving with an Army unit?" I asked.

He said, "I like it fine."

I found out he was from Wilmington, North Carolina, and I had visited there a few times. Then I noticed the restoration schedule on the white board behind me, which also listed the clinic classes and teachers.

"The board looks very organized to me," I commented. *It looks very busy*, I really thought. I then proceeded to the Major's office.

"CPT Patrick, nice to see you again," MAJ Franklin greeted me. We went to her office and started to talk about what has been going on.

"I actually teach a lot of the classes," MAJ Franklin said.

"I saw that on the schedule," I replied.

"The team here takes the enlisted and utilizes them in other ways. This leaves me doing a lot," she went on.

"It all comes down to leadership," I told her.

The Commander of our entire unit was at this clinic at Camp Liberty, where our headquarters were. SSG Sanders, who was in charge of the enlisted at the clinic, was her main assistant. SSG Sanders had the enlisted doing many jobs, though they could have been more involved with the classes.

I told MAJ Franklin to try and talk with the Commander. I showed her our setup at Balad and explained how we had prepared the restoration team at our clinic. I sat in on some of the classes, had chow with the Major, and later we worked out at the gym together.

I stayed about two days then headed back to Balad. I was fortunate to get on a helicopter ride back. Sometimes you may stay longer if transportation is backed up.

Once I had returned to Balad, I told our team Commander what I had seen and what advice I had given to MAJ Franklin. This is what the unit Commander wanted me to do since I had already been deployed and was familiar with the way the clinic operates. I hoped it would help. Little did I know something very critical was about to happen!

Me at the clinic in Balad

CHAPTER 14

Home Issues

"Carol, are you sure now is the time I need to take emergency leave?" I asked. My sister, Nancy, had not been doing well over the last few days. She had been diagnosed with colon cancer and it had traveled to her brain. She was on chemotherapy and had just gotten out of the hospital after experiencing dehydration and falling down the stairs one night, trying to go to the bathroom. I talked Carol into getting Nancy into a nursing home with hospice.

"Yes," Carol replied, "Come home now!"

I knew the time was close. *I hope I can make it all the way back in time*, I thought. These words of the song, "Praise you in this storm", kept playing in my head.

And I will Praise you in this storm
And I will lift my hands
For you are who you are
No matter where I am
And every tear I've cried
You hold in your hand
You never left my side[15]

Praising him in the storm is what I did. I listened to this song over and over.

I cried out to God. He ministered to me. Yes, I did praise him. It really was one of the HARDEST times in my life. He never left me. His is all powerful and capable. I don't know what I would have done if I didn't know the Lord.

I had gone to the PAX terminal, and twice I had to wait because of a mechanical failure on the planes. So at 0300 I made it back and finally got a flight out to BIAP (Baghdad International Airport) at 0600. Since I was going home due to an emergency, I was put on a C130 flight with seven others who needed to get home quickly. The only catch was it was a flight with a "fallen soldier." So we rode with a coffin on the plane. All of us were honored to do so.

I never did get the name of the soldier because my mind was on getting home. Sitting on that flight was very sad, because the coffin made me think of my sister, but faith held me. It was surreal. I knew the days ahead were going to be the hardest for me. Going to Iraq was nothing

---

[15] Hill, Mark, John and Herms, Bernie (2006) "Praise you in this storm". https://Google.com/search q=praise-you-in -this-storm-lyrics.

compared to facing this challenge. I wanted to be strong for my family and to be there for my sister.

The fallen soldier represented the supreme sacrifice, giving oneself for one's country. But I needed to give myself to my family and do all I could to love and serve them during this time. I prayed that God would give me grace to endure this.

We landed in Kuwait, changed into civilian clothes, and got on a plane to the States. We arrived in Washington, DC, at 0830 on May 10, 2009, and I arrived in Cleveland, Ohio, at 1000. A church member picked me up at the airport. We had a quick coffee and then headed to the nursing home.

I entered my sister's room and saw her in her bed. I was happy I made it there to see her in time but sad to see her this way. She was bald from the chemo and had a gash on her forehead from the fall. She knew I was there and called out my name. I hugged and kissed her. She had been crying out in pain, so they gave her more medication.

Brad, her son, was holding her and crying, and most of the family was there. My other sister, Carol, and her husband had spent the night there. I stayed awhile, feeling the effects of flying and the time change catching up to me. I went to church with the friend who had picked me up, and then I went home to bed. It was good to see my natural family as well as my church family.

The next morning I visited my mom. It was so good to see her. A little later I went to the nursing home to stay overnight with my sister. I was in her room, getting unpacked, and then I turned on the TV. Some of my family were there but were in the process of leaving. I saw my unit Commander at Camp Liberty, giving a tour of the clinic, on the evening news!

"Here is where we teach our classes," she said. "This is where the clients sleep," she continued as she pointed to the bunks in the clients' quarters. After the tour, the camera went back to the news anchor, who reported that five soldiers had been shot at a combat stress clinic at Camp Liberty in Iraq!

CHAPTER 15

Unit Tragedy

Earlier that day at Camp Liberty, a Staff Sergeant was at the clinic for an appointment. All of a sudden, a shouting match ensued in one of the back offices. The clients in the waiting room witnessed the Staff Sergeant getting aggravated and belligerent. He threatened to kill himself as he stormed out of the clinic with his battle buddy right behind him. The clinic staff called the Military Police.

Shortly thereafter, the clinic door swung open. The Staff Sergeant had returned! Armed with his battle buddy's M16 Rifle, he started shooting! Three soldiers in the waiting room were struck down before they had a chance to react. The Staff Sergeant also managed to shoot a psychiatrist and a social worker before being apprehended.

Back at the nursing home with my dying sister, I yelled to my family, "I was just there!" I was in shock! I told them, "I visited that clinic at Camp Liberty last week!"

I learned the details the next day. SSG Russell, a forty-four-year-old, who had been on three previous deployments, and who had been at the clinic for treatment, wanted to get out of the Army and be sent home. He claimed he had PTSD and was seen by the social worker and a psychiatrist, both of whom told him he would be better with treatments and medication. He did not like what they said, so he stole his battle buddy's M16, drove back to the clinic, and shot two officers and three enlisted. As a courtesy to the loved ones, who are the first to be notified, the names of the soldiers could not be released.

This news, together with all that was going on at home, kept me awake most of the night. I kept wondering which officers and which enlisted were the victims. Were all of them soldiers in my unit? I would not find out until I returned to Iraq.

My sister, Nancy, kept crying out every few hours when the pain medications ran out. So, I had to get the nurse to come to the room to give her another dose of medicine, which would calm her down for a while. But even as a healthcare worker who has seen a lot, the hardest thing was watching my sister struggle so much. By 0600 (6 a.m.) she was finally quiet and asleep. I nodded off myself.

Nancy's husband, Steve, came to replace me in the morning so I could take a break. The phone rang about 1530 (3:30 p.m.). My sister, Carol, said the doctor was in and it would not be long, maybe twenty-four hours. I went running in the park with my friend from church and returned to the nursing home around 1800 (6 p.m.). Nancy had already passed. I let her husband and three sons remain in the room while I waited outside with Carol and my friend.

The day of the wake was my birthday, though I was glad no one sang "Happy Birthday" because it was one of the saddest days I'd ever experienced, and none of us felt like celebrating. Many of my church friends came to the funeral and watched me deliver the eulogy. One of them sang three songs at the service, including "Rescue" by Eddie James. I needed Jesus to come to my rescue! Where else could I go? [16] This is exactly how I felt. I was numb and in a daze.

The good thing was my sister came to my church when she was first diagnosed and committed her life to the Lord. This, along with support from family and friends, and other officers from the 256th Combat Support Hospital where I drilled in Ohio, helped me get through this difficult time. My mom had a tougher time than I did, though. She had lost one child and was about to lose a second since I was leaving once again to return to Iraq!

---

[16] Eddie, James (2004) "Rescue." https://www.azlyrics.com/eddiejames/rescue.html

CHAPTER 16

Trials in Iraq

"What are they doing?" I asked another traveler after I had landed in Kuwait on my return trip to Iraq. "They are checking us for any fevers from the swine flu," the fellow passenger replied. I was in a line now, and there were masked workers taking everyone's temperatures by sweeping an instrument across their foreheads. It looked like a scene from a science fiction movie. *How weird*, I thought. *If it wasn't for the reality of my deployment, I would have thought this was a crazy dream.*

Back in Balad, forty miles north of Baghdad, I landed at the air base called Joint Base Balad, which hosts 28,000 Army and Air Force personnel. That was where I learned the names of the victims from the clinic shooting at Camp Liberty where I had visited the two officers a week before the shooting. They were MAJ Michael Houseal, 54, from Amarillo, Texas, and LCDR Charles Springle, 52, of Wilmington North Carolina. The enlisted were not soldiers from my unit, but they were getting help at the clinic. They were PFC Michael Yates, Jr., 19, from Fredericksburg, Maryland; SPC Jacob D. Barton, 20, from Lenox Missouri; and SGT Christian E. Bueno-Galdos, 25, from Patterson, New Jersey.

The clinic at Camp Liberty was closed for three months while under investigation, so the staff were reassigned to other teams in Iraq. I had been afraid I would be called to Camp Liberty to help out, but I felt relieved when I learned the clinic was closed and I didn't have to go.

"There are more soldiers coming to the clinic," LTC Batterson said to me after I reported back to work. LTC Batterson was the OIC of the Balad team. He was in his mid-fifties and had a thin physique and balding hair. A psychologist by profession, he was a very calm and fair leader. I was glad to serve under him.

"Some outpatient clients will be coming now. So with the inpatient ones, as well, we will be doing more intakes," LTC Batterson continued. An *outpatient client* comes to the classes during the day and then returns the next day. An *inpatient client* stays overnight for three days. An *intake* is an interview to gather information to better serve the soldiers' needs and assign classes.

"We are going to assign more of the classes to the

OT's so that the 68' x-rays [mental health specialists] can have the time to do more intakes," the Colonial finished.

Great. I thought. "Just what I want, more work." I had two NOV 3's or COTA's (Certified Occupational Assistants) under me. One was SGT Matthews. He was in his late twenties, 5'10", and had a medium build and sandy blond hair. The other COTA was SPC Donalds, a twenty-one-year-old lean guy who was well-liked and had a great attitude. SPC Donalds was being transferred to a prevention team.

"That leaves just two of us right now," I explained to SGT Matthews later when I met with him after the meeting. "When you or I have a day off or go to R&R, it is going to be challenging for us, to say the least. Here's what we will do," I explained further. "Each of us will take turns taking the clients to the gym in the mornings. This will mean three mornings for each of us until we get a replacement for SPC Donalds. Then we will only have to do two days each." We did not go to the gym on Sundays.

"OK," SGT Matthews agreed.

"I will teach stress management and relaxation techniques and take the OT activity class. You can continue to do the classes you have been doing. If we need to substitute for one another, we can change out. Just let me know in advance. Hopefully soon we will get that replacement."

The next day, I arrived at the clinic for the client rounds meeting we had each morning to discuss issues and progress about each soldier in our program. Teaching more classes made the day even longer. At the end of our meeting, we discussed some unit business. LTC Batterson said, "MAJ Franklin will be coming here for few days since the clinic will be closed at Camp Liberty."

I met with MAJ Franklin at Camp Liberty. She was another occupational therapist who served on a restoration team. The restoration teams operate the clinic where the clients stay and classes are taught. "She is here to observe for a while. She will then go visit with CPT Stewart," the Commander told me.

CPT Stewart is an occupational therapist from our unit at Forward Operating Base (FOB) Warhorse, which is a preventative team. The preventative teams have fewer soldiers who provide services to FOB's.

"So I want you, CPT Patrick, to check on her when she arrives. She will be staying in the female bay for a time," the Commander finished. This was where the female clients stayed when they were in the three-day program. We had about eight bunks, so there were empty ones at times. I wasn't the happiest with this information because I now had the added task of serving the Major.

MAJ Franklin arrived when I was busy out-processing a soldier and entering two other soldiers into the clinic program. I greeted her and she got settled. I stayed late to catch up on progress notes that evening.

⬦ ⬦ ⬦ ⬦ ⬦ ⬦ ⬦

"I can't believe it," I said to my sister on the phone later that night when I called her. *This can't be happening.*

"Yes," Carol replied, "Ma was having blood in her stool, and when I took her to the hospital, they did tests and found her spleen was swollen and there was a tumor in her colon. They are going to do a biopsy."

Oh no. I hope this does not mean what I think it means. "Stay in touch," I told my sister. "Email me right away with the results," I reminded her as I hung up. I immediately emailed my church friends and asked them to pray for my mom.

I had to stand in faith and trust God like never before. It was hard being so far away from my family. I did talk to the Chaplain before Sunday service, however, and the worship team I was on at Gilbert Chapel prayed with me Sunday morning. This definitely helped.

The worship team at Gilbert Chapel in Balad

The next day the OIC took me aside and said, "I need you to drive MAJ Franklin to transient housing. She can't stay here any longer since we have female clients here now." It had been a week since the Major had arrived. Now the female bay needed all the beds.

"OK," I replied to the Lieutenant Colonel. When the Major arrived, I took her to the housing unit. She was not very happy and became very upset. I thought to myself, *This is all I need now. It's so busy, and now dealing with this is just too much.*

"I don't want to come back to the clinic or go to lunch with the staff anymore," she cried. I did not expect her to be so shaken up.

"You can volunteer to work at the Air Force hospital here on base if you want to occupy your time," I told the Major.

"No, I don't want to," she countered. I dropped her off and had to return quickly because I had the Lieutenant Colonel's vehicle.

"The Major wasn't too happy," I shared with the OIC when I returned. "She does not want to come back to the clinic at all." The OIC was not pleased with this report.

"I want you to check up on the Major tomorrow and take MAJ Thompson with you."

"Yes, sir," I replied. I didn't know what to expect, and I was hoping it would be better for all of us the next day. The drama department was not short on players. It seemed our unit kept having incidents and issues.

The next morning, MAJ Thompson, one of the current psychiatrists and I, went to see how MAJ Franklin was doing. She was doing better and the two Majors went to a movie on base and then to the PX. I went to worship practice at Gilbert Chapel.

CHAPTER 17

Life in a War Zone

During a sand storm, mortar attacks increase. Four attacks had already occurred earlier that day. Sand storms can last a few days. I was on my way back from worship practice at the Air Force chapel when the alarm sounded. "Indirect fire! Indirect fire! Take cover! Take cover!" I jumped up and ran as fast as my legs would carry me to the nearest bunker. When the all-clear sounded, I headed back to my Chu. While walking, I heard someone call my name. I turned around to see the OIC in his vehicle.

"CPT Patrick, get in!" he yelled. "I have been out checking accountability and knew you were on your way back from the chapel." I got in his vehicle and he drove me back to my Chu.

"Thanks," I said. I was glad I did not have to ride the bus home that night. Later on in the deployment we had to call in only when there was an alarm instead of going back to the clinic for accountability. After five days the dust storm cleared. MAJ Franklin was finally able to travel to FOB Warhorse.

"Yahoo!" I exclaimed one Tuesday morning after I found out SGT Martin had flown into Balad the night before. He was the replacement for SPC Donalds. I was so excited to have more OT help. I spent the morning revamping the schedule. SGT Martin was twenty-two, thin, and very inquisitive. He got re-acquainted with the other staff, and, with the extra help, things went a lot smoother for a while.

One morning on client rounds, LTC Batterson told us, "The intelligence heard Al Qaeda plans to send rockets over the base around 2300 (11 p.m.). So I would like the staff to stay at the clinic overnight." I put a mattress from the female bay on the floor of my office and slept on it. Accountability was taken around 2000 (8 p.m.). Nothing happened that night, but we were prepared.

Another rumor was that Al Qaeda planned to knock down our gates around the perimeter and raid the base. Again nothing really happened, but we needed to remain on alert just in case. One night after work when I was leaving to go back to my CHU, the incoming alarm sounded, and I headed for the bunker. But before I got there, I heard a mortar hit to the right of me. I was shaken out of my boots! After what seemed like an eternity, the all clear was sounded, and I returned to the clinic for an accountability check.

The Chaplain told me on Sunday that the mortar hit 150 yards from the hospital. Some soldiers took pictures of the hole. One soldier had gotten shrapnel in his butt. He ran but did not hit the ground first. The Chaplain said they were using 107mm rounds and that they were Russian mortars. "They fire at the gates and try to hit the hospital," he said.

Joint Base Balad is home of the Air Force Theatre Hospital, which is a level-one trauma center. We have a few defense systems on base called C-RAMs. I have witnessed how they intercept mortars and shoot them down before they hit the ground. It is really a spectacular sight!

A week later, a sand storm had been looming one day, and a Black Hawk helicopter crashed at the airport. Some were injured and one soldier was killed. Our unit gave a debriefing, and we found out SPC Michael Cote, Jr., a twenty-nine-year-old crew chief from Denham Springs, Louisiana, was the victim. He was with the 1st Battalion 52nd Aviation Regiment, Task Force 49.[17] He left behind a wife and new daughter he had only seen once. He had been to our clinic for one of our day classes. I found out later twelve others had been injured.

Another Sunday I was at the PX and had to take cover when the alarms sounded. Two 60mm mortars had

[17] (2009, Sept. 19) The Fallen. 9/19/2009. https://thefallenmilitarytimes. com/armyspc-michael-s-cote-jr/4288825

hit the parking lot. They happened to be duds, which means "a thing that fails to work properly or is otherwise unsatisfactory or worthless,"[18] and I was glad. I called the clinic and made sure they knew I was OK.

— • ✦ ✦ ✦ • • —

The battle at home continued, as well.

"Mom's in the ICU again?" I asked my sister, who I had called from our clinic.

"Yes, she had the surgery, went to the ICU, then to another floor, and now back to the ICU."

"Wow," I replied. "She may not be recovering well because of all the years she smoked." My sister agreed.

"She probably has pneumonia," I guessed. Having worked in a hospital for fifteen years, I knew this could happen. "I will have to request more prayer for her recovery. How are things otherwise?"

My sister said, "OK, I've been paying your bills and checking your condo, no problems there."

"Good." I said good-bye and returned to my life in the war zone!

---

[18] https://www.lexico.com/dud/definition

CHAPTER 18

Daily Grind

The next day was the Army Physical Fitness Test. I knew I could pass, but I did not know if I would pass the weight standard. I had been on leave, so dieting was the last thing on my mind! Plus, I am only 5' 4", so it is challenging to keep the weight off. We headed to the gym and performed sit-ups and push-ups. I did fine. Now for the two-mile run. We were able to use the track next to the gym. This is my favorite part. I love to run!

"On your mark, go!" cried our team Sergeant. I ran at a pace I knew I could keep. It was dusty and hot, but I run better in the heat. I had to run eight laps. I rounded the curves and kept going. My times were called out as I passed by the timer. I made it! I was about two minutes faster than my age standards.

"Now the hard part," I said to myself as I went on the scales. "Oh no! It looks like I am over weight by what? Five pounds! Only five pounds!"

Now I have to be taped, I thought. Two of the female soldiers took my measurements. I wished this was just a diagnostic test, but it wasn't. So it counts.

Later, I had to see the OIC for a counseling statement since I did not pass. This meant I had to lose those extra five pounds before the next PT test in October. Diet time again!

The next day before leaving in the evening, the OIC called me into his office. "I need you and your soldiers to get the progress notes in on the clients the same day. They can't wait until the next day," he told me. It seems my staff was waiting until the next day to write notes on the clients.

"Yes sir," I replied. I was not expecting the next statement. "It would be nice if you helped your staff more by staying off the phone and not watching movies on your computer. You should help more with the classes so your soldiers can get their notes done on time."

Ouch. That hurt! *I am on the phone because I need to know how my mom is doing. If your mom was going through life-and-death scenarios, wouldn't you be on the phone?* This got me wondering. I know they see me through the glass windows when I am on the phone because that is where the phone is. From that point on, I decided I would call home later and use a different phone.

As for watching movies, yes, I watch them at lunch time only and leave the door to my office open. But after my conversation with the OIC, I decided to close it. Maybe this was the reason everyone seemed to know my business. I guess that is what it is like when you are with your unit all the time. Life in a fish bowl. Personally I thought everyone was just getting on each other's nerves. I remembered the book, *Don't Sweat the Small Stuff.* This was a small thing, so I was not going to let it stress me any further. There are more important things in life to be upset about. Pick your battles wisely!

✦ ✦ ✦ ✦ ✦ ✦ ✦

"Wake up! Come on, CPT Patrick!" SGT Fleming, the soldier on night shift, yelled as he shook me awake

"What time is it?" I asked.

"It's 0200, ma'am," the night soldier replied.

"What is going on?" I cried out.

"There is a soldier who needs an intake interview," replied SGT Fleming. Just then I remembered I was on call that week to do nightly intakes. So, I went to my office after talking to the escort who brought the soldier. I found out this soldier had threatened his NCO. He already had two Article Fifteens.

An Article Fifteen is when a commanding officer can punish a service member for a minor offense. It is a non-judicial punishment and may or may not lead to a court martial. The unit proceeded to take away his weapon, and he was brought to the clinic. I entered my office, and the young male soldier, who was around nineteen, came in. I told him to sit down.

"You see," he said, "My wife has cancer and has been in and out of the hospital. I just want to be with her. My unit will not let me return home. I keep having nightmares. I can't stand it anymore. I want out!"

"Well," I began, "you are here for our program. I recommend you attend the stress and anger management classes. The psychologist will give you some counseling, and, if you need any medications, they will prescribe them for you. Make the best of this opportunity. You can talk to the Chaplain, who comes on Thursdays too, if you wish. After you get done with our program, they will reassess. They may still let you go home, even if it is for a week on leave. Don't make it any worse by resisting."

I then entered him into the program and led him to the male bay where he put his things in a locker and went to bed. The next day he was oriented to the schedule and classes.

About a week later when things were settling down a bit, it was time for SGT Mathews to go on R&R. This meant more work for the rest of us, like taking clients to the gym and teaching most of the classes. More stress!

Also during this time, MAJ Franklin returned from her visit to FOB Warhorse. *I don't know if I can take this chaos,* I thought. We had two soldiers from our other teams at our unit too, because they came and went from R&R. The airport is on this base. They flew into Balad and had to wait until their flights were ready before they could depart. We had been putting them up, so to speak, by allowing them to sleep at the clinic while waiting. It was nice to see them, but when we were busy working with our clients, it got crazy.

"Hey, CPT Patrick," MAJ Franklin said, "I like it here the best in Balad, because the food is better and the Bazaar here is great. I have been shopping today and bought some nice things. Want to see?"

"Sure, in a minute," I said during classes. *Boy, it would be nice to just relax and shop,* I thought as I was getting ready to teach again. It really wasn't her fault that her job was visiting clinics since the incident at Camp Liberty.

———— ✦ ✦ ✦ ✦ ✦ ————

"The psychiatrists are leaving!" shouted SPC Owens about a month later.

"Wait!" I yelled back. "I need a picture." I took the picture and then said goodbye to them. Soon we would be getting two more psychiatrists, but we had no idea exactly when they would arrive since it was a war zone and we had to wait on their flights. We would be short on staffing for intakes and counseling sessions. *Great, even more stress! This is getting more intense and exhausting. The daily grind is getting to me. What do I tell my clients about stress? I need a taste of my own medicine. I need an outlet.*

But God provided for me, and it was my saving grace!

CHAPTER 19

An Oasis in the Desert

I loved attending the Sunday morning services and having Christian fellowship. That was my outlet. I felt "normal" again after being in church. I needed it at least once a week to escape the daily grind in the clinic. In the sermon Chaplain Roberts was presenting, he asked, "Why does God have you in the desert?" This was of interest to most of us, for we were all in the desert. I took notes and then reflected on it in my quiet time.

Being in the desert is a time to realize what is important in life and what is not. It is a "time out," so to speak. While on deployment I came to see that commercialism and materialism don't matter at all. Life is simple. Get up;

eat; and go to work, meetings, church, to the gym, and back home. In my case, it was the mission, serving the clients, and my unit.

The military makes sure its service members can attend Sunday services and be with other believers. In Iraq it's interesting to see just how many service members suddenly get spiritual. It is a great opportunity for the Chaplains because all kinds of services are provided in theatre: Catholic, Protestant, Jewish, and Jehovah Witnesses, to name a few. I am grateful that I was part of the contemporary service and that I could be on the worship team.

Our team was there for one another. We prayed for each other's needs. I needed that Christian fellowship, not only because I was in Iraq and so far away from home, but also because of the stress, challenges, and difficulties I had experienced at the clinic. I was about to experience even more. My time in the desert was a time of testing. It showed me what was most important in life. It showed me how to hold onto God and my faith.

Throughout the deployment, Chaplains came and went. God used the weekly sermons to help me get through the hard times. Chaplain Strong spoke on Daniel and the lions' den, Chaplain Worthy spoke on Job, and Chaplain King spoke on making it through the fire. We had six to eight Chaplains that year, but the three I just named are the ones I remember the best. Putting all the names together, a phrase emerged: the King is strong and worthy! It meant that God is enough to see me through!

CHAPTER 20

The Battle is the Lord's

When I went to work the next morning, I saw the OIC talking with a Chaplain. I did not think much of it until they started coming to talk with me.

"This is Chaplain Miller. He heard from the Red Cross there may be an emergency in your family." I didn't want to hear it! I backed out of the room. I knew it was my mom. If she was to go at this point, I knew I couldn't take it.

"No," I said. "My mom can't be that bad. I will not go home for another leave. She will pull through; you will see." I called my sister and she told me that our mom had pulmonary edema and was on a ventilator. I explained to

Carol that it would be very difficult for me to come home again on another emergency leave, so I asked her to keep me posted and to call me only if it looked as though our mom was near death's door.

I asked a nursing friend to check to see exactly how my mom was doing because I knew my friend's word would be truthful. I prayed like never before that my mom would recover. God knows how much each of can handle, and 1 Corinthians 10:13 (NIV) says, "...And God is faithful; he will not let you be tempted beyond what you can bear..." I clung to that verse.

I also kept playing a song I had written that God had given me before coming to Iraq. Part of the lyrics are, *I will Glory in you, my King; I will be safe and secure under your wings; Then in the darkness I can sing, for I'm abiding in you.*[19] This was the truth. It sure did help me when I needed it. 1 Samuel 17:47 speaks about how the battle is the Lord's. He may not deliver by sword or spear, but I can trust Him to deliver me His way.

Just when it couldn't get any worse, a friend from my church at home emailed me and said he and his family were leaving the church! He was the Assistant Pastor! In the email, he explained there was doctrinal error occurring. The Pastor and the other Assistant Pastor were preaching on "hyper grace," which is, in fact, universalism, a belief that everyone will be saved and go to Heaven. This was not easy to swallow because I was very close to my church family. They had just helped me through my sister's wake and funeral. Now to hear this was devastating.

---

[19] Patrick, Andrea A. (2008) "Hungry for God."

I scheduled a phone conversation with the Assistant Pastor and his family. I took notes and came to the conclusion I would have to leave the church too. I talked with one of the Chaplains at Gilbert Chapel about this, and he gave me moral support.

The next Saturday was worship practice. I loved going to practice because when we were singing and playing, I felt so close to God, and that had always reduced my stress. We practiced the song "One Day." It was a dusty night, which meant mortars. Sure enough, we hit the floor, taking cover when the alarms sounded. As soon as the all clear was sounded, we rose back up and continued practice. That's how it was in Iraq.

CHAPTER 21

Clinic Days

The next month, the new psychiatrists came, one of whom I had known from annual training, and the other was a Major who had never deployed before. There was also another psychiatrist who was there just to do research. The OIC had to help the new psychiatrists so they could eventually handle a full caseload, especially since it could get busy fast.

The third psychiatrist, LTC Green, wanted the staff to take her on a tour of the base and the clinic personnel to help her with her research. We really didn't have time to help much, though, because we were running a clinic and needed to help the clients. One time she took the

OIC's vehicle and ran over a cement divide. He was not very happy about it.

"Ways to de-stress are different for everyone," I explained to the clients during stress class one day. "Listening to music is one way to reduce stress. Some people like to read or take a walk," I added.

"What about boxing?" SGT Randal, one of our clients, asked.

"Yes, that's another way to reduce stress as long as you're not angry and pick a fight with the other boxer," I said with a smirk. SGT Randal had a history of not sleeping well and had anxiety and panic attacks. He was at the day program for counseling, medications, and self-help classes.

"Later I will give you some more information about how to relax during the relaxation class," I told him. "It is very helpful to know how to de-escalate from anxiety."

It was 1500 (3 p.m.) so it was time for the occupational activity class.

"Are there any painting kits?" SPC Evans asked.

"Yes," I replied as I opened the cabinet containing all the painting items. SPC Evans was at the clinic because of home-front issues. His wife wanted a divorce. She was cheating on him and using his money to buy unnecessary things. He also had a three-year-old daughter. He had been having trouble concentrating, he had been depressed, and he had been having problems with other soldiers in his unit.

"Painting is a good way to create something. It helps me to relax," I added. PVT Warner was assembling a model car. Wood was also available, and some of our soldiers used it to make two corn-hole boards. They used them with beanie babies until we could order some regular bean bags.

"Yes, I live in Denver, and this is my third deployment," SGT Randal told me the next morning as we headed for the gym.

"I have never been to Denver," I replied. "It is a place I want to visit, though," I liked to talk to the soldiers and get to know them when we walked to the gym in the mornings from the clinic. Sometimes just talking to someone can help people sort their problems out. Some soldiers find it easier to talk to a Chaplain than a psychologist. The Chaplains came to the clinic to teach spiritual health classes and were available afterward if the clients wanted to talk. Seven soldiers were in the program at this time. Four others came only for the day program.

We worked out for an hour at the gym. On our way back to the clinic, we were headed to the DFAC for breakfast when the alarms went off before we got there. So, we had to take cover and head for the bunkers as fast as our legs would carry us!

After the all clear sounded, we headed for chow, but were denied entry until we put on our Kevlar and flack vests since we were under an ongoing attack. So we ended up changing our clothes at the clinic and finally got to the DFAC to eat breakfast.

Each Saturday night I took two buses to get to worship practice at Gilbert Chapel. When I entered the chapel one Saturday night, one of the airmen on our team said, "I wanted to let you know about the drummer at my dad's church. He had a heart attack and died."

The church members prayed for him, and after an hour of being declared dead, he came back to life! He said he was at the throne of God and heard singing in Heaven, but then he was informed that he had to go back to earth. He was healed! We all agreed that was some miracle, and it inspired us as we practiced the worship songs.

⧫ ⬩ ◆ ◆ ◆ ⬩ ⧫

During the rainy season, there are mud puddles galore! Navigating them takes some skill. As I mentioned previously, the mud in Iraq is thick, wet sand that acts as a soft cement. It attached to our footwear like a goopy magnet. I lived in a Chu about two miles from the clinic, and because of the puddles and mud, I, along with everyone else, often had to take the small busses home, so the busses were overloaded.

One evening I had wrecked my boots in the puddles, getting to the bus stop. When the bus finally arrived no one would get off. The people were packed in like sardines in a can! All the windows were steamed. So I walked the rest of the way back to my Chu in the thick, gooey mud. When the mud dried later on it was easier to salvage your boots.

"This morning I need SGT Matthews to take one of our clients to the JAG office. CPT Patrick, you will need to pick up SGT Matthews' classes," the OIC said at the staff meeting.

"Yes, sir," I replied. SGT Matthews was gone longer than I thought he would be.

When the client and SGT Matthews returned, the SGT told the client, "You need to bring your gear to me so I can do an inventory to admit you into the program."

"I will not!" the client suddenly cried out. "The JAG officer did not help me. I am not going to stay here or go into any program." The client started to lash out. CPT Carter, one of the new psychiatrists, ran out to see what was happening. The client took a swing at her, but she ducked just in time to avoid getting hit. The escort who accompanied the client bounced into action. He dove forward, grabbing the client's legs, and took him down, pinning the client to the floor of the conference room. The MP's were called in and took the client away.

"Wow, that was close," SGT Matthews said. "I didn't think he would get that mad."

"We all need to be ready for anything," CPT Carter said. She didn't realize how right she was!

CHAPTER 22

Tensions Rise

"MAJ Travers, our social worker is going to be in charge when I leave for R&R," the OIC declared at the evening staff meeting the next night. I was happy the OIC was going because he was getting a little stressed out. MAJ Travers was a hard-working officer and did not take much time off. He was in his fifties, tall, and had a Hispanic background.

After the Commander left, it was quiet for a few days, and then one morning, "CPT Patrick, MAJ Travers called to me as he came into my office. I need you to stay and do these two exit interviews for me. I am so busy with counseling the clients I am seeing now, I need your help." I had no choice but to stay. The only trouble was I had never done exit interviews, so I didn't know what to do. I taught classes and mediated groups. One-on-one counseling was not my area of expertise. So, I wasn't very thrilled about this.

That night at my Chu, I had the weirdest dream. I dreamt I was trying to get to the stadium with a group of people to watch the Cleveland Indians game. One of the leaders of our group told us to climb this fence, so we did. The field was wet and muddy. We ran through water and waves and I turned around and ran back out. I saw the score board. We were losing by three runs.

Later I went to a house and found a bedroom with a giant bed in it. I tried to sleep, but builders came to fix the roof, so I had to wait to sleep.

In another moment, I found myself at a retreat. We were to go to a meeting and I fell asleep in the hotel room. I got up in the middle of the night because I heard noises. I tried to find my way back, but I ended up in another hotel room. I got into someone else's bed, and then I woke up. I concluded my dreams were telling me to get some rest!

◆ ◆ ◆ ◆ ◆

It had been a while since I had called my sister. So I called after work when it was morning in the States. My sister was not short on words.

"Really?" I said on the phone.

"Mom is talking nonsense."

Oh no, I thought.

"They drained her lungs," she told me.

"Thoracentesis," I said.

Carol continued, "Now she is a little confused."

"This could be a metabolic problem," I said when I heard that.

"They took a CT Scan to see if it was a stroke," Carol added.

So much to have happen all at once, I thought. *I wish I could just go home now!*

At the clinic a few days later, I was told the Major wanted to see me, so I walked to his office. He was finishing up with a client and looked tired as usual.

"Yes, MAJ Travers, what do you want, sir?" I asked.

"I need you to do some intakes because it is busy and the OIC is gone on R&R. I would like you to be on call Sunday afternoons. I need help with crisis statements too." I did not like to work on Sundays because it was my only day off. I was also wondering how busy the new psychiatrists were. I found out one of the psychiatrists wanted to lead the clinic, but Major Travers would not let him.

I talked with the NCO of our unit later and explained to him that the Major was asking me to do duties I had not done before and were not in my line of work. The NCO said to me, "I am making a list of things the Major is doing while the OIC is gone to give to him when he returns." I thought this was a good idea, so I made my own list for the NCO.

Anytime a group of people spend long hours working together, personalities surface and working as a team

115

becomes a balancing act. How each person affects the others determines success or stress. At this point in our deployment, stress was at an all-time high. The tension was so tight I could feel it in the air. It was like waiting for a pressure cooker to explode. I remembered a comment one Air Force nurse made to me before she left Iraq to return home: "This place can suck the life out of you." She was right!

Again it was time for two of our psychiatrists to go. This meant that MAJ Travers would need more help until the replacements came and the OIC returned. It was so stressful with so many demands and challenges. *What more could happen*? I asked myself. The answer to that came quickly!

A few days later we had a visit from our unit Commander! She was there because she had heard about the difficulties our team members were going through. The rumor was our team was too disciplined.

Each of us shared with the Commander privately about the issues we were having. I told her some of my concerns but did not elaborate. I did not want to rock the boat, because if I did there would be changes, which meant new staff and rotations.

It takes a while to get used to new personnel. It is easier to just go with what you already have and know. Besides, our deployment would be over soon, or so I thought. Little did I know that even more bad news for our unit was about to come!

CHAPTER 23

Ft. Hood Events

A shooting occurred at the Ft. Hood SRP, Service Readiness Processing Center, the announcer on the television set said. I had just woken up and turned my television on in my Chu. I was at Ft. Hood myself just one year earlier obtaining the necessary medical clearances for my deployment to Iraq.

November 5, 2009, started like any other day at Ft. Hood, one of the largest military complexes with about 40,000 troops, and home to the Army's 1st Cavalry Division in Killeen, Texas. Soldiers were standing in line, going through medical preparation stations. Each soldier had to be cleared to go to Iraq or Afghanistan with their unit.

A loud sound broke the silence! Soldiers then heard someone yelling, "Allahu Akbar!" Shooting rang out, and soldiers started falling like shooting gallery targets being hit at an amusement park! A medical worker hid under her desk in terror as she heard more shots fired around her. Chaos ruled as the shooting continued. One soldier felt a sting as a bullet hit him in the arm and he fell. Three soldiers in line were gunned down and lay helpless on the floor. The shooter was standing on top of a desk firing wildly in every direction.

One soldier managed to crawl out of the building. He later returned to help a few others out, fortunate not to have been hit himself. A police woman was in the area, heard the radio report, and did not hesitate to respond. She charged in, shot the attacker four times, and was hit in the process. According to reports, the shooting took less than ten minutes.

The announcer on my TV continued, "A Major Husan, a psychiatrist working at Darnell Hospital at the base in Ft. Hood, shot and killed twelve military personnel, one civilian, and injured thirty-one others." I could not believe what I was hearing! I knew soldiers in the unit Husan was deploying with, so I desperately wanted to know who had been shot.

At the beginning of my deployment, I was at home when I heard about the Camp Liberty tragedy. Now I was in Iraq, hearing more bad news, but it was back in the States at Ft. Hood. I really believe it was God protecting me.

That day at the clinic I read in an article online that said, "Hasan 39 had listened to soldier's tales of horror. Now the American-born Muslim was facing imminent deployment to Afghanistan."[20]

I learned later that MAJ Husan was to be deployed with the 467th Combat Stress Control Detachment. He didn't want to serve in Afghanistan because he was Muslim. He wanted out of the military, but they would not release him. One of the psychiatrists at our clinic worked with him at Walter Reed. Of the twelve military personnel killed, three of them were from Husan's unit, the 467th. I found out two others were from the unit that was to replace ours! They were from the 1908th Combat Stress Control.

Who were the soldiers killed in the 467th? Did I know them? Would this delay the 1908th from replacing us in Iraq? Would this mean staying in Iraq longer? I don't know if I can take this much longer. What more could possibly happen?

I found out the names of the fallen soldiers. Those from the 1908th Medical Company of Independence, Missouri, were: LTC Juanita L. Warman, 55, from Havre De Grace, Maryland, who treated individuals with PTSD; and CPT John P. Gaffane, 56, a psychiatric nurse from San Diego, California.

---

[20] (2009, Nov. 6). Major Nidal Malik Hasan: Soldier's Psychiatrist who heard front line. *The Guardian Stories* 11/6/2009. https://www.theguardian.com/world/2009.nov/06/nidal-malik-hasan-fort-hood-shootings1.

The soldiers from the 467th Medical Detachment, in Madison, Wisconsin, were Major Libardo E. Caraveo, 52, from Ciudad Juarez, Mexico, a psychiatrist with a private practice in Woodbridge, Virginia; and CPT Russel G. Seager, 51, a nurse practitioner from Mount Pleasant, Wisconsin; and SSG Amy S. Krueger, 29, a mental health specialist from Kiel, Wisconsin. A member of our unit, who was a psychiatric nurse, knew CPT Seager.

I did not know any of the fallen soldiers killed that day. I do know, however, that just like me, they were professionals serving their country. This hit so close to home for me. It could have easily happened to my unit. It made me think about how vulnerable any of us are!

I also knew the Commander and a psychologist who were both in the 467th because I had been to Iraq with them in my first deployment. I am grateful to God this didn't happen a year earlier when I was there!

CHAPTER 24

A Turn for the Better

Meanwhile back at home, I learned that my mom went to Regency Hospital, a long-term care hospital, before heading back to the ICU. This meant she may not make it!

The pressure continued to mount at the clinic as MAJ Travers, the acting OIC, wanted the staff to do all kinds of odd jobs.

"I wish the OIC was back," I said to SGT Matthews. "He would put an end to the craziness."

Finally the OIC returned, and it was better at the clinic for a time.

The day arrived for the PT test! This time I did great and my weight was down. I did not have to be taped (measured). I passed! What a relief!

A few days later I was on the phone with my sister.

"Really?" I asked my sister.

"Mom is out of ICU. The vent is off and she is doing better."

"Praise God. That is great news!" I said, smiling.

My mom's birthday was coming and I had planned to send her a gift basket. I was happy that I could order and send it to the States from Iraq, over the computer. I asked my sister to take a picture of my mom in her hospital bed, and Carol emailed it to me. I then printed it out and put it on my desk.

The 1908th team finally arrived in November. I met the OIC and a psychiatrist. Both were female soldiers, and it was nice to talk with them. I oriented them to the restoration program.

CHAPTER 25

Holiday Ending

Our unit was almost ready to return home, but we had to stay until after the holidays. This would be the second holiday I would spend in Iraq. This was a solemn holiday, having experienced so much tragedy with this deployment. The 1908th CSC (Combat Stress Command) was coming to replace us.

They had just been through a difficult time, losing unit members to the terrorist attack at Ft. Hood. Even after they were debriefed, they still wanted to come and serve in Iraq. We had a visit from MG Chang. He had been at Ft. Hood and had met the unit that was coming to replace ours. He was there to reassure us that the 1908th would still be coming.

They arrived in November. The day they came, I showed the new team Commander, LTC Nelson around. She was an occupational therapist. LTC Ivanson, a psychologist, was with her. It was nice to be with other women officers. I had been the only one while I was in Balad.

A bus took us to the Air Force Chapel for the Christmas Eve service. Since I had served there for most of my second deployment, I knew the Chaplains and the worship team members. In the traffic circles were some trees decorated with ornaments and Christmas lights. It was odd seeing Christmas decorations in the desert. All of a sudden LTC Ivanson started to cry.

"This will be my first time away from my family during the holidays," she sobbed.

We started to sing Christmas songs on that bus. Even the Iraqi driver sang with us. It seemed to calm the Lieutenant Colonel down. I could not help but remember another Christmas five years ago in Iraq where we sang Christmas songs in that bunker.

The Christmas Eve service was good. The sermon was done by a Chaplain I knew well after having talks with him during my stay in Iraq.

Christmas day I sang in the church choir. We had a great meal at the DFAC, and no mortars were fired that day.

The Sunday after Christmas I led worship since a few

soldiers in our band had redeployed home. The last song we sang was "Rise up and Praise Him."

After the service a one-star General came up to me and said, "Thanks for playing 'Rise up and Praise Him.' I had wanted to hear that song since we played it back at my home church."

I was blessed to hear that. Chaplain Brown preached a sermon titled, "The Desert in the Desert." It was about encountering Jesus. It sure was true for me. I had encountered Jesus there!

Now it was on to redeployment and out-processing.

CHAPTER 26

Back to the States

"What?" I cried when I heard we were going to redeploy at Ft. McCoy in Wisconsin. We had come to Iraq at the beginning of our deployment after training at Ft. Hood and were supposed to redeploy there.

"Oh no. I can't understand why we have to go there. For one thing, it is January, and that means going from the desert to snow! That isn't a good transition. It would be better to go to Ft. Hood since we are familiar with that base," I muttered to one of the soldiers in our unit. Ft. McCoy is the base for Army Reserve units to train and now it was to be the base for redeploying. Still it didn't sit well with most of my unit.

We went to Camp Virginia from the PAX (passenger) terminal in Balad. We stayed in tents for a few days and then went through customs. Having to unpack all of our gear was challenging.

"I hate when this happens," I said to SGT Donaldson, who was in line with me. "It is so hard to repack again after everything is removed."

"You got that right," he replied back.

Finally we were on buses heading to the airport in Kuwait.

"Hurry up and wait" is an Army saying. Sure enough we were on the buses at 2200, traveling to the airport. When we got to the airport, we waited in the buses for an hour before we boarded the plane. We sat on the plane another hour before we finally left at 0330 (3:30 a.m.). We were on our way to Germany. It took five hours. We had a layover of two hours. Then we were on to Iceland with another layover that lasted three hours. This is why we learned how to sleep anywhere anytime we could.

As we came in for a landing at Ft. McCoy, all of us gathered at the plane windows as we coasted into the terminal on the Ft. McCoy airstrip at 1334 (1:34 p.m.). It was sunny, but it was also 1 degree Fahrenheit with a wind chill factor of -20, so the ground around the aircraft was a sheet of ice. It took a lot of skill to negotiate around the ice and snow on the way to the terminal.

"Oh, look. A band is playing for us," I said as I looked out the plane window. A small crowd of people was standing in the cold, cheering and singing.

"This is nice," I said. It was a great welcoming ceremony.

Later in the barracks at Ft. McCoy, I reconnected with other members of my unit that I had not talked with in a quite a while. This deployment had been difficult for everyone. I heard a lot of stories about what had happened at the clinic at Camp Liberty, though I may never be able to confirm them. I, along with everyone else, was so ready to get out of there. I did not a want to stir the pot, so I kept to myself and did what I was told to do.

The next day we began out-processing, which lasted a week. There was six inches of snow on the ground with a wind chill factor of -20! I was glad I had my parka.

I heard later that a soldier from our unit had fallen and broken his arm.

Most of us were burnt out. There was no party, though we did have the awards ceremony, and MG Chang was present. I was awarded the ARCOM (the Army Commendation Medal) for the second time.

My flight home consisted of going to Minnesota, then to Chicago, and finally home to Cleveland. It would have been easier to fly directly to Cleveland, but this is the way the Army contracts commercial services. At that point I was glad just to be going home!

CHAPTER 27

Home for Real

I arrived home Saturday, January 9th, exactly one year since I had left for Iraq. I came into Cleveland around 1430 (2:30 p.m.). On our approach into Cleveland was a frozen Lake Erie outside the airplane window. From the arid desert to the frigid winter, I was home sweet home!

Two friendly faces, my sister, and my friend, Patty, were at the airport to welcome me. I went out later that evening to eat with another friend from church. Now I needed to get back into the routine of my life.

I arrived on Saturday and attended church the next morning. It was bittersweet. I was happy to be reuniting with my church family, but sad knowing I had to leave them. I met with the pastor's wife and explained that I could not stay because they were espousing a doctrine (hyper grace) that was not biblical. I then gave her a book on the biblical approach to grace.

Though she didn't express it, I knew she was upset that I was leaving. When the others at church found out I was leaving, they thought it was because I'd had a tough time in Iraq. I attended a midweek prayer meeting at the assistant pastors' house until I found a new church home. He was the one who had left the church a few months earlier.

I met a friend I knew at Walmart one day after I returned home. I found out she had married when I was on my first deployment and that her house had blown up from a gas leak! Her husband was questioned and taken to jail in connection with the incident. I felt bad for her. I used to visit her and her mom at that house, and now it was gone.

My mom had been doing OK since I returned. It was a miracle to see her at home. She had been in the hospital on and off since the fall and had just gotten home in December. My cousin told me later that my mom did all she could to survive because she wanted to make sure I returned from Iraq safe.

About two to three weeks after she had returned home and I had seen her, she became depressed again. My mom can make it through a very difficult time and then, after it is over, go into a depression. We had to take her to the hospital again, and then she went to the nursing home for a while to have her medication adjusted. My occupational therapy friend worked at this nursing home, and it was nice to know my mom was being treated well in therapy.

I was able to get a vacation in prior to returning to work. In February I went to Florida and visited all the amusement parks. It was chilly but nice to see NASA, the Epcot Center, and Universal Studios.

In those first months home, I transferred Army units and started drilling at the Reserve Center in Twinsburg, Ohio. I couldn't handle another deployment with my old unit in Indianapolis. I needed a change after returning from such a trying year in Iraq. I had deployed with the same unit for two different tours and thought it would be best to start anew in a different unit.

In March I first attended drill with the detachment. In August I attended a weekend drill at Camp Sherman in southern Ohio where we qualified at the rifle range. We drove down in Humvees and stayed in the barracks there. The evening before we went to the firing range, I set up practice with a computer simulation of the rifle range. When we went to the range the next day, it was nice getting to fire rounds again. I passed and was even able to shoot with the pistols too.

Two other officers I knew well did not want to qualify, so they loaded rounds into magazines all day. I preferred shooting. The supply Sergeant, SGT Penn, fitted us with gear and ammunition. It was a nice weekend.

SGT Penn was in charge of the rifles and the armory. Usually two soldiers were assigned to maintain the armory at the Reserve unit. However, this time SGT Penn was alone, and one night he rigged a rifle in the armory to take his own life. I found out about this at the next drill meeting. We had a debriefing, and the ones conducting it were from my old unit that I deployed with. It was good to see the team that was sent, but it was under such sad circumstances. I did not know SGT Penn long, but he left a wife and children behind.[21] Being on the receiving end of the meeting was certainly different.

I returned to my occupational therapy job at the hospital. A lot had changed in a year, and it took a little adjusting to get back into the working routine. The staff morale was low during this time, which reminded me of Iraq. I did not want anyone controlling me after a year of taking orders, so I probably wasn't pleasant to be around. I didn't think I came across as difficult, though.

My boss and assistant boss called me into the office one day and confronted me about being angry all the time. It took me by surprise, but my wanting to be free from authority came across to others as being angry with them. *Please give me a little time to adjust. If you were where I was for a year, you would feel the same way.* I needed a grace period to work things out.

Being at home is no different when it comes to difficulties and challenges. Whether in Iraq or at home in the States, a tragedy is a tragedy. A trial is a trial, just like being in the battle zone. The disasters and challenges continue, no matter where you are. The question is are you prepared to handle the difficulties? Who or what do

---

[21] (2010, Aug. 27). Obituaries. *Cleveland Plain Dealer*. 8/27/2010. https://obits.cleveland.com/us/obituaries/cleveland/name/thomas-penn-obituary?pid=145027119

you turn to for help? Who or what do you depend on? I turn to faith. I praise God I made it. He was and is with me every step of the way.

I retired from the Army Reserve in November 2011. My mom was with me for two years after I returned and passed away from stomach cancer in 2012. I was blessed to have her to return to after such a challenging time. On, December 8th, 2011, President Obama pulled out all the troops, from Iraq, and my team OIC retired from the reserves in March 2012.

A year after I returned, our unit met again at a yellow ribbon conference. We were reunited with members of our unit, the unit that replaced us, and the unit that went to Afghanistan. We had counseling sessions, and our family members were invited to attend. This is one way the Army helped us reintegrate back to post-war life and make peace with our experiences in Iraq.

CHAPTER 28

Freedom from Battle Fatigue

My fatigue from battle did not come from experiencing physical combat. It was from my personal battle zones, which, in Iraq, consisted of the daily grind at work, home, family health issues, deadly shootings, living in a war zone, and redeploying home.

My freedom from the stress of battle came from knowing and trusting God, prayer, Christian fellowship, music and worship, knowledge of stress management, and coping skills. As a Christian, I knew I needed God's help to get through. This is the grace of God. Grace empowers us and it is God's mercy to us. In the battle zones of Iraq, I needed to depend on him while doing my part.

Scripture shows that we work with God in a partnership. He does his part, and we do ours. Ephesians 4:22 says, "…you lay aside the old self…" and verse 24 says, "…put on the new self, which in the likeness of God has been created for righteousness and holiness in the truth" (NASB). We are responsible to have faith and be obedient to God.

God gives us the strength to serve as we trust him. God had prepared me for the time and season of serving in Iraq. All the gifts and talents he has given me were used when I was there. That was what helped me get through my deployments under such difficult circumstances. I don't know what I would have done without Jesus.

Even after all I endured, I am grateful to have served in Iraq. I learned how important it is to have faith and a relationship with Jesus. I experienced being an occupational therapist in a war zone and was educated in self-help skills. I now understand the balance of work, rest, and recreation. It's in the "little things" that lessons are learned and life is lived. I appreciate the unit I was in and the other professionals I worked side by side with day in and day out. Selfless sacrifice is one of the Army's values, and it was exhibited in Iraq. It is also a Christian value, and I was grateful for the other Christians who served with me.

The second deployment was the most difficult because so many negative life events occurred. I felt that deep ache inside from having lost my sister. Daily, I worried about my mother in the hospital far away from home. *Would I lose her too?* Then there was the day-to-day stress at the clinic. My church issues and the Ft. Hood tragedy just added fuel to the fire.

I held on by having faith. It is hard not knowing, but that is where faith comes in. It sure was tested and tried, but my experiences during that time made my dependence on God stronger. It showed me *I can* trust him! James 1:2-4 sums it up: "Consider it all joy, my brothers *and sisters*, when you encounter various trials, knowing that the testing of your faith produces endurance. And let endurance have *its* perfect result, so that you may be perfect and complete, lacking in nothing. " (NASB).

Faith begins by admitting your fears to God and others, bringing it out to be dealt with instead of holding it in. Holding it inside just leads to more anxiety and stress. It is a choice to actively trust God during the storms.

Courage, moving forward in spite of fear, is another Army value. The storms will come. Who is with you during the storms? I kept 2 Thessalonians 3:3 with me while I was overseas: "But the Lord is faithful, and He will strengthen and protect you from the evil one." (NASB). I know God kept me safe.

I invite you to receive Christ for yourself. Nothing is more important, no matter what you face in life. Are you ready to face conflicts, crises, and traumas? Who do you trust or rely on? Who do you run to? I say go to God. He is able, and he can be trusted. If you want to know him, all you have to do is ask.

Receiving Christ involves turning to God from self (repentance) and trusting Christ to come into your life to forgive you of your sins and to make you what He wants you to be. Just to agree intellectually that Jesus Christ is the Son of God and that he died on the cross for your sins is not enough. Nor is it enough to have an emotional experience. You receive Jesus Christ by faith, an act of your will. God knows your heart and is not as concerned with your words as he is with the attitude of your heart. The following is a suggested prayer:

Lord Jesus, I want to know you personally. Thank you for dying on the cross for my sins. I open the door of my life and receive you as my Savior and Lord. Thank you for forgiving me of my sins and giving me eternal life. Make me the kind of person you want me to be. In Jesus' name, Amen.[22]

---

[22] How to Receive Christ. https://www.ficm.org/how-to-receive-christ.

STUDY GUIDE:
Leader Notes

This study guide can be used individually or in a group. If used in a group setting, start the group and end with prayer time. Keep discussions confidential to the group. Each chapter has questions pertaining to the content. There are many questions. The group may focus in on the questions that stand out to them. Others should listen as people share and then open up discussion to the group. A scripture verse is printed for each chapter. There are additional scriptures suggested to look up if time permits or for a homework assignment. When looking up verses using different translations is helpful. The study guide is meant to be used to address and answer hard questions and issues with the word of God. Resources are included in the back of the book for more severe issues and problems that may need professional help. I pray that this book and study guide will benefit others going through difficult times. Remember God is the source of our strength. Psalm 46:1-3 (NASB).

STUDY GUIDE:
Questions for the Chapters
(not all chapters have questions)

Chapter 1-2: 1. How would you respond if you had to be on 'guard duty' by protecting a building, person, or child from a dangerous situation? Would you feel fearful? Brave? Prepared or not?

"The Lord is my light and my salvation; Whom should I fear? The Lord is the defense of my life. Whom should I dread? "(Psalm 27:1-2, NASB). Ps 91: 1-16, Ps 56:3, Phil 4:6-7.

2. None of us are guaranteed tomorrow. One contract worker and one service member were killed instantly when a mortar hit their building while they were at work.

Are you prepared to face eternity? Do you know Jesus as your Lord and Savior?

"I have been crucified with Christ; it is no longer I who live, but Christ lives in me; and the life which I now live in the flesh I live by faith in the Son of God, who loved me and gave himself up for me" (Galatians 2:20, NKJV). Eph 2:8, John 14:6, Rom 5:8, Ps 9:10, Rom 8:28.

3. If you were to travel far from home on a mission trip or serve in the military are you ready to sacrifice all to God and trust Him with your life?

"Therefore I urge you, brothers and sisters, by the mercies of God, to present your bodies as a living and holy sacrifice, acceptable to God, which is your spiritual service of worship" (Romans 12:1, NASB). Is 41:10, Ps 28:7.

Chapter 3: 1. If you were to be in a dangerous situation and needed to take cover during a lightening storm or natural or man-made disaster, would you be prepared to face it and know what to do?

But if any of you lacks wisdom, let him ask of God, who gives to all men generously and without reproach, and it will be given to him" (James 1:5, NASB). Jos 1:9, 2 Tim 2:4.

2. Could you save someone in an emergency? How would it affect you if someone you knew tried to commit suicide? How could you be available to support others affected by this kind of trauma?

"I can do all things through Christ who strengthens me" (Philippians 4:13, NKJV). Matt 5:4, Ps 34:18, I Pet 5:7, John 14:27, Gal 6:2, 2 Corin 13:7, Matt 11:28, Ps 23:4, 2 Thess 3:3.

Chapter 5: 1. SPC Smith felt guilty because he believed he failed his battle buddies. Has this happened to you? Do you feel like you let someone down? How did it make you feel? Were you able to reconcile the guilt? What did you do?

"If we confess our sins, He is faithful and just to forgive our sins and to cleanse us from all unrighteousness" (1 John 1:9, NKJV). I John 4:18, Rom 5:1, 5:27, Ezek 36:26-27.

2. SPC Gerard was open and ready to change his life. He received Jesus as Lord and Savior. Are you ready to serve Jesus and let go of the old life and embrace the new life in Christ?

For God so loved the world, that He gave His only begotten Son, that whoever believes in Him should not perish, but have eternal life" (John 3:16, NKJV). Col 3:10, Eph 4-2-24, 2 Cor 5:27.

3. SPC Begin wrote a poem in which he mentions pain and suffering Have you had a difficult season.? What helped you pull through? Did you use art, music, poetry, nature to help you? These are part of God's creation.

"When Thou saidst, Seek ye my face; my heart said to you, Thy face, Lord, I will seek" (Psalm 27:8, KJV). James 1:2-4.

Chapter 6: 1. If you have lost loved ones around you how did you make it through the difficult time? Did you seek support from other loved ones and family, friends? Did you help others while you were going through grieving?

"God is our refuge and strength, A very present help in trouble. Therefore we will not fear, though the earth should change, And though the mountains slip into the heart of the sea; (Psalm 46:1-2, NASB). I Pet 4:12-19, I Corin 10:13, 2 Corin 12:9, John 16:22, I Thes 4:14.

2. Did you learn something from the experience? Were you willing to seek out support? Did you apply what you learned? What do you do when life is hard?

"Seek the Lord and His strength, Seek His face continually" (Psalm 105:4, KJV).

Chapter 7: 1. Have you served on a one day mission or a week long mission trip? How did it make you feel after serving others less fortunate then you? Did you have to sacrifice time/money to go? Was it worth it? Why? What advice would you give someone who wanted to go on a mission trip?

"Go therefore and make disciples of all the nations, baptizing them in the name of the Father and the Son and the holy Spirit, teaching them to observe all that I commanded you; and lo, I am with you always, even to the end of the age" (Matthew 28-19-20, NASB).

Gal 6:2, Heb 13:16, John 15:12, Phil 2:4, Rom 12:13.

Chapter 8: 1. Do you have a dream or vision for your life? Does it involve helping others? Do you need special training or schooling? Are you willing to sacrifice to do this? Could you visit people from another country and be comfortable with their cultural differences? Would you be willing to dress differently and show respect by following different customs? How far should you go?

"Do nothing from selfishness or empty conceit, but with humility of mind let each of you regard one another as more important than himself; do not merely look out for your own personal interests, but also for the interests of others. Have this attitude in yourselves which was also in Christ Jesus, who, although he existed in the form of God did not regard equality with God a thing to be grasped, but emptied Himself, taking the form of a bond-servant, and being made in the likeness of men. And being found in appearance as a man, he humbled Himself by becoming obedient to

the point of death, even death on a cross" (Philippians 2:3-8, NASB). Jer 29:4 Is 58:11, Ps 32:8, Ps 37:23, Heb 13:16.

Chapter 9: 1. How can you survive if you have to be in a dangerous area? How can you be prepared? How can you use wisdom to avoid and get through a dangerous situation?

"Trust in the Lord with all your heart, And do not lean on your own understanding. In all your ways acknowledge Him, And He will make your paths straight" (Proverbs 3:5-6, NASB). Prov 14:16, Prov 22:3, James 3:17, Prov 3:13-18.

Chapter 10: 1. Have you served with a Pastor in your church? How was the experience? Did you learn something? Was the Pastor a good example-role model? How would you define role model? Has God answered a pray for you and provided something you needed? Did you reach out to others in a new study group? Did you make them feel welcome? Have you ever given something to someone that God directed you to? Have you ever prayed for someone you know who needed prayer? Share a time God answered and provided for you after you prayed.

"Be devoted to one another in brotherly love; give preference to one another in honor, not lagging behind in diligence, fervent in spirit, serving the

Lord" (**Romans 12:10-11, NASB**). Gal 6:2, Phil 2:4, I John 5:14, James 5:15.

Chapter 11: 1. Sress-How do you define it? Have you had it? What did you do about it? How can you change for the better if you are dealing with (anger, guilt, jealousy, un-forgiveness, poor sleep, poor diet habits?)

"He who had my commandments, and keeps them, he it is who loves me, and he who loves me shall be loved by my father and I will love him and will disclose myself to him" (John 14:21 NASB). Prov 3:4-6, Phil 4:6, Matt 6:34, Lk 12:25-26, James 1:2-4, Ps 94:19, Prov 19:17.

Chapter 12: 1. Did you ever have to go someplace you didn't want to or weren't ready for? How did you get ready? Were you able to make it through? Did it affect your family, friends? How? What did you learn about yourself after you went through this?

Not that I have already obtained it, or have already become perfect, but I press on in order that I may lay hold of that for which also I was laid hold of by Christ Jesus. Brethren, I do not regard myself as having laid hold of it yet; but one thing I do: forgetting what lies behind and reaching forward to what lies ahead, I press on toward the goal for the prize of the upward call of God in Christ Jesus" (Philippians 3:12-14, NASB). Heb 13:5, Ps 73:23-26, Rom 8:38-39, Matt

28:20. Chapter 13: 1. If you had to visit someone you didn't want to could you still be nice and helpful to that person? Could you make the best of a difficult situation?

"Remind them to be subject to rulers, to authorities, to be obedient, to be ready for every good deed, to malign no one, to be uncontentious, gentle, showing every consideration for all men" (Titus 3:1-2, NASB). I Pet 1:22, Eph 4:32, Phil 4:2, Lk 9:23-24.

Chapter 14: 1. If you had been through a tragedy or lost someone, how did you cope? Were you willing to receive help and give help to others? Did you go through a grieving process? How long did it last? How did you recover?

"Bless the Lord, O my soul; And all that is within me, bless His holy name. Bless the Lord, O my soul, And forget none of His benefits; Who pardons all your iniquities; Who heals all your diseases; Who redeems your life from the pit; Who crowns you with lovingkindness and compassion;" (Psalm 103:4, NASB). John 6:22, Ps 34:18, Jos 1:9, Prov 22:4, Prov 12:1, Ps 9:9.

Chapter 15: 1. Could you resume school or work after a difficult time? How did you make it? Did you get help from God or others? (explain). What advice would you give someone that has been through a hard time?

"Rejoice always; pray without ceasing, in everything give thanks for this is the will of God in Christ Jesus concerning you" (1 Thessalonians 5:16-18, NASB). I Pet 5:7, Ps 145:7, Matt 6:33, I Thess 1:16-18.

Chapter 16: 1. Have you ever had stress build up at work or school? Was there any consequences; physically, mentally, or spiritually? How did it get better? How did you cope? Did you turn to prayer, worship the Bible, faith?

"Again, the kingdom of heaven is like a treasure hidden in the field, which a man found and hid; and from joy over it he goes and sells all that he has, and buys that field" (Matthew 13:44, NASB). Is 40:29, Matt 11:28-32.

Chapter 17: 1. We all live in a world where we don't know what can happen in a given day. Is there an area where you struggle? Do you have a strong area? How do you improve in the areas that are hard for you? What do you do to change? Are you resistant or ready to change?

"All discipline for the moment seems not to be joyful, but sorrowful; yet to those who have been trained by it, afterwards it yields the peaceful fruit of righteousness" (Hebrews 12:11, NASB). Heb 12:1, 2 Tim 3:16, 2 Corin 5:17, Rom 12:2, Lk 6:43-45, 2 Corin 4:16, Phil 1:6.

Chapter 18: 1. Have you been in a tough situation for a long period of time? Did you learn patience? How can you be peaceful when you are in a job or situation with constant tension, stress?

"Are not five sparrows sold for two cents? And yet not one of them is forgotten before God. Indeed the very hairs of your head are all numbered. Do not fear; you are of more value than many sparrows" (Luke 12:6-7, NASB). Gal 6:9, Col 3:12, Ex 14:14, John 14:27.

Chapter 19: 1. Have you ever been burnt out or exhausted? What did you do? How did you come out of it? What are areas that helped you cope? How did you balance these daily?

"Draw near to God and He will draw near to you. Cleanse your hands you sinners; and purify your hearts, double-minded" (James 4:8, NASB). Is 26:3, Col 3:15, James 3:18.

Chapter 20: 1. Have you been in a relationship where you have gotten on each others' nerves? Did it come to a turning point? What did you do? Did it lead for a change for the better?

"And He said to him, 'You shall love the Lord your God with all your heart, and with all your soul, and with all your mind'. This is the greatest and foremost commandment. The second is like it, 'You shall love your neighbor as yourself' (Matthew 22:37-39, NASB).

Prov 10:17, Prov 9:7-9, Prov 15:32, Prov 19:20, Matt 22:37-39.

Chapter 21: 1. When an ordeal was over and life balanced, how did you feel? Did you ever go through a major experience and learn something from it that changed you? Would you go through it again if it changed you for good? Why does God allow trials and suffering? Can you see his hand in it? Can you give your wounds/hurts to God? Can you surrender your problems to him? What did CPT Patrick do when going through tough times? Did this help? Why or Why not? What would you do?

"And we know that God causes all things to work together for good to those who love God, to those who are called according to His purpose" (Romans 8:28, NASB). 2 Corin 1:3-4, Rom 5:3-4, Rom 8:18, 2 Corin 4:17.

Chapter 22: 1. CPT Patrick had to pick up the pace and work more when others were on leave. Did you ever have a job or project where you had to work longer hrs? Did it affect your sleep or concentration? What did you do about it? How did you cope?

"Let your light shine before men in such a way that they may see your good works and glorify your Father who is in heaven" (Matthew 5:16, NASB). Ex 15:26, Prov 17:22, Jer 33:6, Is 58:11, I Corin 6:19-20.

Chapter 23: 1. CPT Patrick's replacement unit had a trauma occur and were delayed in coming to Iraq. When you hear bad news about friends or relatives, how do you manage when you are far away and can't be there for these friends or relatives?

"Do not be anxious about anything but in everything by prayer and supplication with thanksgiving let your requests be known to God. And the peace of God, which surpasses all comprehension, shall guard your hearts and your minds in Christ Jesus" (Philippians 4:6-7, NASB). Heb 11:6, I Tim 6:6, Hab 3:17-18.

Chapter 24: 1. 'Burn out' can happen to anyone. There is a time though when things finally turn around. CPT Patrick had this happen when she, passed the PT test, found out her mom was transferred out of ICU and the new unit was coming to replace the 55th. How would you respond to the good news, after having so much turmoil?

"Shout joyfully to God, all the earth; Sing the glory of His name; Make His praise glorious" (Psalm 66:1-2, NASB). Phil 4:4, Ps 118:24, Neh 8:10.

Chapter 25: 1. It was almost time to return home for the Combat stress team. They still had to train the incoming unit. The new unit had issues because of loss of their commrads coming into Iraq. Just when CPT. Patrick thought it would be a little less hectic it turned out that the new unit needed a lot of encouragement. It was around Christmas time too. So more time and energy was needed. Where could you find strength if you had a hard year and just when you thought it would get easy you had to do more yet?

"Yet those who wait for the Lord will gain new strength; They will mount up with wings like eagles, They will run and not get tired, They will walk and not become weary" (Isaiah 40:31, NASB). Prov 14:29, I Corin 13:4-5, Rom 12:12, Ps 37:7.

Chapter 26: 1. It was now time to return home. Yet there was another hurdle to tackle. The 55th was scheduled to re-deploy at Ft. McCoy in Wisconsin instead of Ft. Hood in Texas. What this meant was EXTREME weather. Re-deploying in January! Going from the desert to sub -zero temperatures was a challenge. One soldier fell off of a truck and broke his arm. There was a blizzard, along with exhaustion, long flights and then NO party. How would you feel? What would you do?

"See to it that no one comes short of the grace of God; that no root of bitterness springing up causes trouble, and by it many be defiled;" (Hebrews 12:15, NASB). Rom 12:15, Ps 27:14, Ex 14:14, Ps 30:5, 2 Tim 4:2, 2 Pet 3:8.

Chapter 27: 1. Finally home. Trouble follows in the next few months and it still feels like CPT. Patrick is still in the war zone. A friend has their house blow up, returning to work after being away is challenging, and a soldier from the reserve unit commits suicide. How would you handle these situations after thinking it may easier back home in the States?

"Therefore, since we have so great a cloud of witnesses surrounding us, let us also lay aside every encumbrance, and the sin which so easily entangles us, and let us run with endurance the race that is set before us, fixing our eyes on Jesus, the author and perfecter of faith, who for the joy set before him endured the cross, despising the shame, and has sat down at the right handle of the throne of God" (Hebrews 12:1-2, NASB). 2 Tim 2:11-13, I Corin 1:9, Ps 89:8, Deut 7:9, Ps 145:13-14.

REFERENCES

New American Standard Bible. (1995). https://bible.com/version/100_nasb_1995-new-american-standard-bible-nasb-1995

New American Standard Bible. (1977). https://bible.com.version/100_nasb_1977-new-american-standard-bible-nasb-1977

MILITARY RANK ABBREVIATIONS

PVT-Private

PFC-Private First Class

SPC-Specialist (similar to Corporal)

SGT-Sergeant

SSG-Staff Sergeant

SFC-Sergeant First Class

NCO-Non Commissioned Officer

1st & 2nd LT-Lieutenant

CPT-Captain

MAJ-Major

LT.COL-Lieutenant Colonel

COL-Colonel

Team Commander- Local

Unit Commander-Entire unit

LDCR-Lieutenant Commander

MILITARY ACRONYMS

BIAP-Bagdad International Airport

CHU-Containerized Housing Unit

COTA-Certified Occupational Therapy Assistant

CSC-Combat Stress Command

CSH-Combat Support Hospital

DFAC-Dining Facility

FOB-Forward Operating Base

ICU-Intensive Care Unit

IED-Improvised Explosive Device

JAG-Judge Advocate General

MP-Military Police

MWR-Moral Welfare Recreation

NOV 3-COTA in Military

OIF-Officer in Charge

OT-Occupational Therapy

PAX-Passenger Terminal

PR-Public-Relations

PT test-AFPT Army Physical Fitness Test

PTSD-Post Traumatic Stress Syndrome

PX-Post Exchange

SRP-Soldier Readiness Processing

R&R-Rest and Relaxation

91 X-ray-Psychiatric Aide

HOW GOD SUSTAINS/ PROVIDES

1. He plans ahead of us. Ps 31:15, Ephesians 2:10.

2. He provides support for us. Phil 4:19, Ephesians 3:20.

3. He give us Favor and Protection. Ephesians 1:11, Ps 5:12, Proverbs 3:3-4, Ps 6:1.

4. Prayer. Ephesians 4:6, I John 5:14-15, John 15:7.

5. Day to day signs. Ps 91:15, Rom 8:28.

6. The Word of God. Hebrews 4:12, Ps 119:105.

7. Faith (when all else fails) Trust. Proverbs 3:5, Ps 56:3, Isaiah 43:2.

RESOURCES

PTSD:
https://www.militaryonesource.mil/
https://www.mightyoaksprogram.org
https://www.woundedwariorproject.org

Grief:
https://www.helpguide.org>grief

Compassion Fatigue:
https://mhanational.org>compassion-fatigue-empathy-burnout-health-care-workers-which-it

Suicide/military:
https://www.veteranscrisisline.net

Suicide:
https://suicidepreventionlifeline.org

Re-entry:
https://pesresearch.org
Cantrell, B.C., Dean, C. (2005) *Down Range to Iraq and back,* Word Smith Publishing, Seattle, Washington

Depression:
https.//www.nami.org>depression
https://www.ficm.org

Family counselling:
https://www.chrisitanfamilysolutions.org

Stress management:
https//www.nami.org>your-journey/individuals-with-mental-illness/taking-care-of –your-body/managing-stress